A Listener's Guide to Free Improvisation

A Listener's Guide to Free Improvisation

John Corbett

The University of Chicago Press
Chicago and London

John Corbett is a writer, producer, and curator based in Chicago who has written extensively on jazz and improvised music. A regular contributor to *DownBeat* magazine, he is the author of several books, including *Extended Play: Sounding Off from John Cage to Dr. Funkenstein* and *Microgroove: Forays into Other Music*.

The University of Chicago Press, Chicago 60637
The University of Chicago Press, Ltd., London
© 2016 by The University of Chicago
All rights reserved. Published 2016.
Printed in the United States

25 24 23 22   4 5

ISBN-13: 978-0-226-30177-8 (cloth)
ISBN-13: 978-0-226-35380-7 (paper)
ISBN-13: 978-0-226-34746-2 (e-book)
DOI: 10.7208/chicago/9780226347462.001.0001

Library of Congress Cataloging-in-Publication Data
Corbett, John, 1963- author.
    A listener's guide to free improvisation / John Corbett.
        pages cm
    ISBN 978-0-226-30177-8 (cloth: alk. paper)—ISBN 978-0-226-35380-7
(pbk.: alk. paper)—ISBN 978-0-226-34746-2 (e-book) 1. Improvisation
(Music) 2. Music—Performance. I. Title.
    MT68.C658 2016
    781.3′6—dc23   2015030232

♾ This paper meets the requirements of ANSI/NISO
Z39.48-1992 (Permanence of Paper).

Contents

Preface

Most of us grew up listening to songs. Gobs of them. On the radio, in our cars, on our stereos, in movies and commercials, at the supermarket, in video games, around a campfire, in church or synagogue or mosque, at karaoke bars, when our mothers tucked us in at night. Songs gave shape to our lives. They have been our soundtrack, an ever-changing mix tape of songs. We've heard so many songs that we've become experts at listening to them. Generations of us have. We know how they work. Nobody needs to explain them. We know what kind of rhythms to expect, what kinds of forms they might take, how a melody will function as a vehicle for lyrics. Songs are not a mystery.

Of course, great songwriters are there to under-
mine that assuredness by writing songs that out-
strip our understanding and expectation. But
they're teasers, the songwriters. They know how to
tweak the formula just enough without blowing it
up. The songs stay songs, somehow. That's part of
their power. Shake it, but don't break it.

Maybe I'm wrong and you grew up listening to
classical music. Or your parents were into experimental music. Or you grew up someplace where
music doesn't come packaged up as a song—a rural
part of Jupiter, perhaps. In any case, you learned to
listen and expect certain things. And, fess up, you
heard a lot of songs anyway, figured out how to tap
your toes and sing along like the rest of us.

Encountering so many songs has made us in-
tolerant of certain things. We've become, and I
mean this without judgment, *inculcated*. Our musical indoctrination gave us the tools to recognize a
song and to expect that when civilized people were
making music, that's what they'd produce. Most of
the time, that's great. The song is an amazing frame
for music making, insanely versatile, hence its

popular appeal. But for the purposes of listening to improvised music, anticipating a song is actually a hindrance. For a person weaned on song-fare, it's helpful to unlearn those expectations, to prepare a wee bit for something with different fundamentals from the ones we're used to.

As a fan of improvised music and as a critic and presenter as well, I've noticed that newcomers often experience certain obstacles—blockages that it seems to me a little guidance could alleviate. Mainly, it's the residue of all those songs. When listeners don't hear components they recognize, the elements that make sense, they have a hard time warming to the sounds. First off, they expect words. Instrumental music is a hard-and-fast wall for many people who primarily want to hear text set to music. Those folks are probably too far away; they'll never jump the fence. But even adventurous listeners often expect songs. When they hear music that doesn't have choruses and verses or a hummable and memorable melody, sequences of chords arranged to build and/or dissipate tension, and, more acutely, music that doesn't have a consistent beat, that's a barrier. And after a few tries, they might just give up, even after an earnest shot at listening. It's understandable. If you're not encountering and evaluating the things you know how to recognize and judge, then either you (1) think everything unfamiliar is always fantastic or (2) get turned off and eventually think the whole enterprise is worthless.

So, with a remedial ear, I propose this slim volume, *A Listener's Guide to Free Improvisation*, with a select offering of things to listen for, a few ways to listen, several broad contexts in which improvisation might be observed in the wild, and some thoughts on advanced audition for the experienced improvised-music-goer.

What Is Improvised Music?

Improvised music is music made using improvisation. Simple enough. In this book, unless otherwise specified, the term is used in its purest form, sometimes referred to as free improvisation, freely improvised music, free music, spontaneous music, or instant composition, in which improvising alone and no other means like using a previously written score, or remixing, or otherwise monkeying with the time in which the music is taking place—is utilized. Lots of improvisors use hybrid techniques, and most players can move between free improvisation and other kinds of what is sometimes referred to more broadly as creative music, but plenty of them specialize in plain old unadulterated free improvisation.

When you mention freely improvised music, people often have something specific in mind. I've had folks say: "Sure, but they improvise *on* something, right, like chord changes or a melody or something?" Nope. No scores. No memorized tunes. Making it up as you go along, often in groups, sometimes alone. For our purposes, it's easiest to start there.

Some folks are put off by what they assume will be the impenetrable complexity of improvised music. It can be complex, no question. But it's not complexity like watching someone work a calculus problem. It's more like watching a flock of birds swoop and dip and soar, wondering how they know to turn without crashing into one another, which one is signaling to the others and by what means, and how they all land together.

Improvisors come from all walks of life. It's an international art form, with significant contributors from North and South America, Europe, Asia, Africa, and Australia. It has no official hierarchy or administration, is not housed in an academy or industry. All disagreement tends to be worked out in the music itself, rather than by any outside force like a council or a board or a committee. The music is performed in a multitude of settings: bars, clubs, cultural centers, festivals, coffeehouses, bookstores, university concert halls. Often associated with jazz, it is frequently programmed in jazz contexts, as an adjunct to other kinds of jazz activities. I have attended performances of improvised music in every imaginable situation, from train stations to squats to philharmonic halls, but the single most informative event in my personal education was an eleven-day festival I attended in Holland in the early '90s. A total immersion like that—sixty concerts in just over a week—was life-changing. It pushed me from the periphery to the middle of the music, made me listen more carefully. By the end, I'd observed so much action up close and personal that I had a better sense of what constituted the pedestrian and what could be counted as extraordinary in free improvisation.

Free improvised music has a small cadre of supporters, some of whom are in for the long haul, some of whom participate intensely for a while, then either take a break or opt out. Peter Stubley, who established and tends to the amazing European Free Improvisations website (efi.group.shef .ac.uk), has the kind of crazy dedication that improvised music has engendered. Now and then, it has its own publications—*The Improvisor, Signal to Noise*—but most of the time when it appears in a preview or review or feature article, it's in omnivorous magazines like *The Wire* or local alternative newspapers. Now and then the *New York Times* covers a concert. It's a marginal interest of jazz magazines. But you have to actively look for free improvised music; it's not likely to tap you on the shoulder. For everyone involved, there is precious little money in it. Improvisors either (1) hustle for work all the time; (2) actively pursue other kinds of commercial music; (3) have a day gig; (4) are independently wealthy.

Free improvisation has its own complicated history, emerging as a distinct genre in the mid-1960s out of American jazz and experimental music and European contemporary music. It has its heroic figures, its villains, a whole crew of pioneers and cowboys and cowgirls, settlers, tycoons, brother-versus-brother clashes, sheriffs, and libertarians—a regular Wild West saga. Early purveyors included free jazz figures Cecil Taylor, Milford Graves, Albert Ayler, and Sun Ra; members of the Association for the Advancement of Creative Musicians (AACM); guitarist Derek Bailey; saxophonists Peter Brötzmann and Evan Parker; drummers Han Bennink, Paul Lytton, Paul Lovens, John Stevens, and Tony Oxley; pianist Irène Schweizer; and bassists Peter Kowald and Barry Guy. Many synoptic versions of the history have been written, but there has yet to be the definitive tome surveying the genesis and development of improvised music. This is not that book. This book is a guide to listening to improvised music. I have purposefully tried to refrain from lots of name-dropping and historical reference, an off-putting tendency amongst chroniclers of the music, in order to try to treat the subject in a more general and easily accessible way.

Introduction

Improvised music is open to everyone. Experience has taught me this. It is not a mystery cult, esoteric language, or secret handshake. It needs no decoder ring. Sometimes the music's supporters show their devotion—as do lovers of all kinds—by trying to protect its honor. Cloaking it from the meddling misunderstandings of outsiders and keeping it for themselves. There can be a cliquishness to concerts of improvised music—the priestly class of cognoscenti drawn into a circle, comparing notes on the latest releases, bests and worsts listed incessantly, opinions spoken in geeky shorthand with the haughty ingrown patois of the comic store salesman or the fist-pumping, high-fiving, statistic-spouting semaphore of the sports aficionado. They're doing that because they dig it so much they can't contain their enthusiasm. If you work at it, they might let you be part of their circle. But who would want to be?

Alas, enmeshing improvisation in some sort of cryptic codebook is the wrong tack. It takes no highly specialized training to understand improvised music. That's one of its meatiest joys: anyone can come to it. Unlike classical music, in which a caste of academics is officially charged with the music's interpretation and a full course of study might provide insight into one composer's oeuvre. Unlike jazz, with its more informally organized but no less fervent gatekeepers, who count bars and monitor harmonic progressions and listen for clever substitutions and transpositions, penalizing those who break the form and awarding gold stars to those whose approach extrapolates on convention with great individual style and panache. In our case, a degree is not required.

It may not be a requirement, but specialized

training of any variety—not only musical—can in fact be applied to the apprehension of improvised music. Some have applied their PhD in quantum physics, say, or their knowledge of cognitive psychology, the schooling patterns of fish, the customs of traditional German brewmasters. Folks with good long-term memories can hear certain aspects of a performance while others enjoy being completely lost in the moment. Restless people with short attention spans will experience trouble, but then maybe the activity of patient listening will help with that. Of course, people who have improvised themselves can hear a lot in the music that laypeople might not, but that's hardly an obstacle. If you listen carefully, the music is yours. All you need are attention, basic observation skills, time, patience, and a little imagination. That's basically it.

Learning to listen to improvised music is like learning to bird-watch in the sense that

1. Anybody's eligible: you don't have to be an ornithologist or musicologist.

2. You don't have to know how to fly or how to play.
3. The more you do it, the better your skills.
4. Field methods that you figure out on your own are equally worthy.
5. Close attention is richly rewarded.

A basic rule of thumb: all interpretations are valid, but some are better than others. Neophytes will come up with some fresh observations, but I stick to the notion that experience + research = a better understanding. Some bird-watchers are compelled to learn as much as they can about specific birds: what they eat, where they migrate, the normal range of sizes, what dance they do when they mate, other aspects of behavior. Others just want to look for them, to check species and subspecies off their life list. One approach isn't more or less valid, but if I wanted to know something about a particular variety of bird—more, that is, than *That's one right over there, that one on the branch, see it?*—I'd go to the insatiable bird nerd rather than the eagle-eyed bird spotter. Knowledge is power? Yeah, sure, I guess, but more to the point knowledge is *inter-*

esting, exciting, not boring. The more I know, the more I want to know. The more I hear, the more I want to hear, the more I want to know about what I hear. You get it: the circle of knowledge is the circle of not-boring.

Part of that is just plain normal, applicable to anything: the unexamined life and so on. But part of it is endemic to improvised music. Think of this: onstage you have someone whose music you're listening to at that moment, but that person has been onstage playing music many times before that moment, trying all the while to make something fresh and engaged and to keep from needless self-repetition; so your experience in the moment may be that the music is fresh and exciting because you've never heard it before, but then if you see this group of musicians multiple times, you hear the deeper ways that a particular performance may be fresh and exciting (or stale and dull) because of how it relates to all those other times. Just like a birder seeing a meadowlark for the first time, thinking, *That's amazing,* then seeing a few more and realizing it's not such a big deal.

When Europeans visit the States, they're always so bedazzled by squirrels—*Look, over there, there's another one!*—because they have no squirrels back home. Context is king in the amazement department. Being amazed by something you've never seen before is less significant than being amazed by something with which you're very familiar. My wife constantly amazes me. That says more than being amazed by someone I've just met. I know her better. The amazement is way deep.

The bird-watching metaphor is helpful to a point. Most field guides presuppose a static object and a set of traits by which it can be identified. *Reptiles and Amphibians of North America. Flowering Cacti of Northwest Texas. Fanged Insects of the Belgian Congo.* But this is a different situation. I am not suggesting that improvised music is a static object, nor do I have any interest in compiling a definitive typology or even a schematic template for identification. Taxonomies are reductive and exclusive; improvised music is expansive and inclusive. Improvised music is a dynamic object, constantly changing. In these ways, it's perhaps a terrible candidate for a field guide.

But a field guide can be used in different ways. You can approach it pragmatically to ID particular flora and fauna. Or you can read it for more general tips on how to go a-looking. A field guide can help you figure out how to be ready to go into the woods, can give you a framework for observing once you're out in the woods, maybe even help you get over an inhibition about venturing into the woods. A framework, a chassis, a scaffold, some tips, a dram of encouragement—that's this book. The rest is on you.

Preparing to
Go into the Field

1. Take nothing.
No binoculars (or opera glasses) necessary. Recording devices and cameras are distractions that keep you from listening attentively; leave it to the professionals. Cell phones are a nuisance, not just for the listener but for everyone around them; sitting next to somebody texting at a concert is like having a television on at a bar—the light of the phone is a magnet that attracts a curious-minded person's built-in eavesdropping mechanism, causing them to pay rapt attention to something they don't care about in spite of themselves. I've been told that in the early '70s a special brand of idiotic

audience member brought saxophones to jazz festivals, thinking that because the music was so free they could join in. Please. None of this. What you do require: ears, eyes, brain, drink. That's about it.

The point is to bring as little as possible *in your head*. Try to just leave it all at home. Of course, for the intermediate or advanced listener, knowing the history and the various factions and the geographical distribution are all part of the listening process. That becomes part of the excitement, figuring out what's at stake in a specific concert based on what you know about what's come before. Knowing context is essential to the sustained enjoyment of improvised music. To start with, it's important just to come ready to observe. And simple, unobstructed observation is a luxury in our action-packed lives. I have spent many evenings at concerts I'd looked forward to—even ones I organized myself, really great, important ones—and found myself thinking about work or worrying about something I forgot to do or daydreaming. Again, there's a place for all that—flip to the "Advanced Techniques" section for some ideas. But if your first task is to try to figure out what's going on in the music, you have to pay attention to it. Direct attention. As if you were defusing a bomb. Imagine you've got those red and green and black wires in hand, ready to cut one of them, but which one? Not a good time to be mulling over grocery lists or imagining great comeback lines you missed. You've got to stay focused. Lives depend on it.

2. On second thought, take a notebook.

I know it sounds nerdy. But it's really helpful. At a festival I was reviewing early on, I noticed other journalists taking notes, thought I'd give it a try, and though I don't do it all the time anymore, at the beginning it was a great help. It's like taking notes at a lecture—you can't rely on your memory to be complete or accurate, and sometimes your impression in the moment is fleeting and scoots away for good. Unless you've written it down. So overcome your vanity, grab one of those little Moleskine dudes, as small as possible, and mark the date and the players at the top of a page. You think you'll remember. You won't. I've unearthed notebooks from twenty-five years ago that remind me of gigs that I'd totally forgotten. Not only that, but they refresh my memory of little noteworthy events in those concerts that, a quarter century later, I could hardly expect to recall. When I see them on the page, though, it's a mnemonic device; and as often as not, I can reconstitute the ancient music as if it were water hitting Tang—like those specialists who memorize *The Odyssey* in its entirety or a series of non-sequential numbers. That's what improvised music is often: an odyssey or a series of non-sequential numbers. Jot down some observations, some mileposts, musical monuments, what someone looks like when they're playing, feelings of boredom or elation, anything you notice. Nobody else will see your scribblings, so don't worry about being elegant or writing full sentences or even making sense.

3. And a pen.

Notebook's no good without it.

4. And a watch.

A timepiece is helpful. As an artifact of the way it's made, improvised music has a special relationship to duration; time becomes super-relativized in the process of listening to folks improvise—it expands and contracts. Sometimes a watch is needed just to see how long the music's been going, to check how long it feels against how long it's "actually" been going, as measured by the less malleable measure of clock time. It's helpful to note the length of a piece or a set or a whole concert, or even an intermission, if its length seems significant. Anyway, a watch is also an aid in being sure that the bar owner's not going to shut the concert down for going past 2 AM or that you're not going to be late for the babysitter.

Range and Diversity

Free Improvisation

Free improvisors are by nature migratory creatures. They range far and wide, and are common from the United States and Canada to Europe and Asia, with communities in Australia, and occasional sightings in Africa and South America. First identified in the United States and several northern European countries (England, Holland, Germany), free improvisors once roosted locally, but they have now established themselves far from their home berths. Joe McPhee, for instance, who was at one time hyper-local—performing in the small-ish American city of Poughkeepsie, New York—

ventured out and established a base in France, working with a cadre of French improvisors. Likewise, German Peter Brötzmann began performing in the United States in the late 1970s, with the advent of lower-cost airfares, and has forged long working relationships with many American musicians. Freely improvised music is the first thoroughly transnational musical art form, its identity inflected by the various intersections and cross-pollinations engendered by all this migration.

Structured Improvisation

Coexistent with free improvisation, occupying precisely the same habitat, structured improvisation is often mistaken for its counterpart. There is frequent interbreeding between these species, even in a single concert. However, there are some typical markings that can help distinguish structured improvisation from free improvisation:

1. Players looking at sheet music on music stands.
2. Unison activity (i.e., multiple players starting or stopping simultaneously; several players playing

the same melody; more than one player executing a tricky rhythmic pattern in tandem).

3. A conductor standing at the front of the stage, cuing players or directing activity.

4. The bandleader announcing the title of a piece before or after they play it (freely improvised music is only ever named when it is being released as a record, and then often grudgingly).

Free Jazz

With its ancestors in North America and subsequent strains thriving in Europe, free jazz is also difficult to distinguish from freely improvised music. Indeed, some references treat them as part of the same species, and some free improvisors identify themselves as jazz musicians, while some of the Europeans decline to call what they play jazz out of respect for the African American tradition. Here's what people tend to mean when they say "free jazz":

1. Driving rhythm with great forward momentum, usually unmetered.

2. Screaming and shouting horns, especially tenor saxophones.
3. Minimal thematic material, sometimes none.
4. No cycles of chord changes; harmony limited to one chord, if any.
5. Long-form dramatic arc.
6. Optional round sunglasses.

Noise Music

Noise music is a species appearing most frequently in Japan and Scandinavia, with examples sighted less frequently across North America and Europe. Sometimes made using free improvisation as a method, noise music is a distant descendant of heavy rock and tape music (also known as *musique concrète*). It tends to eschew all conventional musical material—melody, harmony, pulsed rhythm—in favor of electronic sounds generated by various means, including synthesizers, electric guitars, and overdriven or mistreated microphones. Frequently employing drone as a baseline technique, noise music can be long and gradual or shorter and song-like with extreme outbursts of high-energy sound. Someone might be screaming. There is probably distortion. It is very loud. *What?!* Loud, it's very loud!

Improv

I'm a purist, at least when it comes to nomenclature. I *never* use the abbreviated form of improvisation. Improv is for improvised comedy, a particular and separate artistic activity. Some of the great comedians are incredible improvisors, not only within the domain of "improv," but all the time, in daily life, on a talk show, at the gas station. Some use scenarios and characters, like Richard Pryor and Andy Kaufman did, and others get into a zone and seem to be able to riff on anything that comes their way. Groucho Marx was legendary for the snappy retort, which is a specialized kind of improvising.

Thinking about improv in the context of improvised music brings up something worth sorting out, though. There's a basic mandate in improvised comedy (and theater), something called the "yes, and" rule. This guideline says that when improvising with others, you should never say "no." Instead, whatever it is that they throw at you, you have to accept and run with it. *Wow, when did you grow ears made of caterpillars?* Last week, don't you like them? *Sure, but they're eating your hat.* I know, but I didn't like that hat anyway. *I gave you that hat!* For my birthday, I know, and I never told you how much I disliked it. And so on. The concept is that if you say "no," no matter how dorky or uninteresting the premise, you break the flow, and the flow is what keeps the audience engaged. I would argue that this is exclusively an artifact of the spoken arts, not music, and that in freely improvised music it is possible, maybe even necessary, to sometimes say "no." Without "no" there isn't any friction, and without friction you basically have new age music. New age music is all "yes." And, to my ear, that's a much bigger "no."

Fundamentals

Rhythm:
The Hurdle

The hardest thing for new listeners to deal with, in my experience, is rhythm. Growing up with a regular beat of one kind or another in virtually every piece of music they've enjoyed—depending on how adventurous they've been—most listeners have to grapple with the fact that in improvised music there's a very good chance that there's going to be no steady pulse, no continuous 4/4 or 2/4 or waltz or 6/8 or even anything as exotic as seven or nine or eleven. There's no reason these things can't appear at some point, but it's unlikely they're going to last the length of a piece, for instance. A drummer may decide to drop a walloping backbeat or some light swing or a metronomic tap into free-flowing interplay, but the music doesn't presuppose the rhythm. In theory, it can't, if it's really improvised. Presuppositions are checked at the door.

Metrical rhythm has a specific function—several, in fact—but one of its functions is to provide a sense of regularity. In other words, it's the music's grid. Against a steady rhythm, anything can be plotted, even the craziest and most unhinged of sounds. I know a few people who are fans of really aggressive, wild, totally out rock, who can't stand free jazz or improvised music. It's the rhythm. They want the grid, the plotting, something to measure the weirdness against. Without it, they feel lost, adrift, as if there's nothing at stake. I also like to experience the contrast between a steady rhythm and something completely bananas. That juxtaposition is exciting, and for some, myself included, it's been a necessary step in the process of feeling comfortable listening to music with non-metrical rhythm. A bit of a safety net.

So what to do in the absence of a beat?

The first thing is to relax. Not to clutch. Breathe.

Admit to yourself there's not going to be a steady pulse. And then begin to pay attention to other things about the music. Like does it seem to move or stay in one place? That's a fundamental observation, whether the music has momentum or remains static. Often within a single performance, this will vary. The rhythms will ebb and flow: things will get hitched to a post and suddenly grow still, or they'll burst out of the gate, break into a trot, maybe a gallop. In improvised music, speed equals velocity, not tempo; it's a matter of feeling a tidal pull rather than counting beats per minute.

I suggest listening to a group without a drummer as a way of trying this out. Drumming is overdetermined. We expect it to lay down the beat, manage the time; we look to the drummer to know what's going on with the rhythm. (Matter of fact, in some music, like jazz, this function is actually the business of the bassist, even though the drummer is known as the timekeeper.) In improvised music, drummers have gone in many directions—some even call what they do "multi-directional percussion"—and to great lengths to open up other possibilities. There's a history of non-metrical drumming in improvised music. As I've said, some improvising drummers have no compunction about bringing the beat, many doing so effectively and without totally dominating the proceedings. (Imposition of a steady beat for a long period in a piece of freely improvised music has a tendency to make everything refer to it, so it eliminates much of the openness of the setting and in effect makes a unilateral decision about the direction of the music. Something like playing "Happy Birthday" or "Chopsticks"—a magnet thrown into a bunch of metal flakes. An extreme measure, experienced improvisors know to use it judiciously.)

In any case, it's a helpful exercise to find a group with no drummer, more akin to a chamber ensemble, and then try to hear what's happening rhythmically. How would you describe the music: slow, medium, or fast? What gives that impression? Density of activity? Can there be dense music (lots going on at the same time) that feels slow? Can there be spare music (a note or sound here and there) that feels fast? Remember that everything is rhythmic, not just a beat. Whenever there are two events separated in time, there's a rhythm. And when you get a whole bunch of things happening, there's the potential for shifting velocity, or overlapping and conflicting velocities, lots of complex rhythmic activity, a whole lotta shakin' going on. Try to figure out: Is one person playing fast, or is the whole of the music fast? How is the feeling of speed created? How consistent is the rhythm? Does it slip and slide all quicksilvery, or does it stay more or less even?

Ekkehard Jost's description of rhythm in Cecil Taylor's work is useful here. He poses a question: Since metrically based swing is the motor of so much jazz, how can motion be created without meter? In Taylor's case, Jost says, it comes from what he calls wavelike activity. He specifies: This means that the music has a tendency to go from a low dynamic to a high dynamic (soft to loud) and at the same time to go from fewer to more notes in a given span of time. So you get swells in volume calibrated with crests in speed. He plays without a pulse but with a definite sense of forward motion. If you want, check out Taylor's solo music to hear what Jost means. His explanation is pretty persuasive, though it's basic and reductive and doesn't really account for much else of value in the rich music.

Listening to music without a steady pulse, you take on the role of code breaker in training: you hold up your stethoscope to the music, working to make sense of something that's complex and irregular, deciphering scrambled code in an asymmetrical or uneven expanse of sounds. It's easy enough to deal with regular patterns—repetitions, cycles, series—so think of this as a challenge to train your brain to understand more organic sounds, ones that don't repeat over and over.

What you trade for the security of the beat is all of these possibilities. You just have to listen for them. The potential for rhythmic ingenuity in improvised music is immense. But it's the first hurdle for a new listener. Once you relax, let down your guard, and pay attention to all the minute rhythmic details—the flux, the freeze-frames, the tasty timings—you can move deeper into improvised music. If you cling to the desire for a beat, you'll forever stand at the front door.

Duration:
Another Hurdle

I'm sitting here, but I could be doing something else. Something productive. Gads, look at the time, I really must be getting home. I thought they were scheduled to go on at 8:00; it's already 8:14. Where's my phone? Maybe somebody's trying to reach me. . . . Wow, that music was great, but another set? When will I have time to alphabetize my CDs? What the hell? Do they think I'm made of time?

We have developed a subtle semiotics of paranoia that betrays our fear of losing time. If we're not careful, you know, things *take* time. How long did it *take*? We are possessive, protective of our "quality" time. It's valuable. And when it's over, it's been *taken*, stolen, pilfered. Or maybe, like money, it's been *wasted*. You're *wasting* my time. *Stolen moments. Hey, bud, do not make a move for my time—I'll cut you!*

OK, so the second thing you have to relax about is duration. In other words, how long will this go on? If you're listening to songs, you have a pretty good idea, unless it's a Yes album or an ad nauseam narrative nautical ballad, that it's going to last a few minutes and be over, followed by the next one. If you're listening to live improvised music, you have no such assurance. In fact, you really don't know how long it will go at all. And neither do the musicians.*

The funny phrase coined for duration in these circumstances is "real time." As in "real-time improvisation." This begs the question, naturally, of "unreal time," which I suppose would be anything that alters one's experience of a given time span. Like TiVo or time shifting. Recording, overdubbing, cutting, and mixing—these are conventional musi-

---

*When freely improvising, players may discuss the time frame in advance, but they tend to do so in general terms like "a short one."

cal activities excluded from the real-time improvisor's realm. Songs that we hear on the radio, for
instance, are often assembled out of lots of disparate and non-coincidental moments, put together
to feel like a single time segment. Real-time improvisation is unedited. The music is consumed as it
is performed, apprehended live in the moment of
its creation. Milk straight out of the cow's teat—so
fresh, so real.

The reason the phrase "real time" is funny,
though, is that duration is not so simple. The
notion of real time in performance suggests clock
time, the reality of the sweep of the second hand,
as if any two swatches of music that went on for
the same number of minutes and seconds would
feel like they lasted the same amount of time—
which isn't true. Listening to music in the moment is often profoundly elastic, and a concert can
condense into something that zips by in a flash or
stretches out into near infinity. Without many of
the usual markers, it's hard to know where you are
in time, where you've been, and especially where
you're headed.

So here's the second major hurdle. Newcomers

to improvised music find themselves without their usual navigational tool, the beat, and to compound that they are also without their handy map, a given or implied duration. It's not hard to understand how off-putting this can be, how lost an unfamiliar listener can feel. Rather than thinking of it as a matter of not getting lost, I prefer to think of it as an attempt at staying found.

The aversion to indefinite music comes from a basic fear: the irrational sense that things will never end. With the exception of very unusual concerts that are specifically durational in nature—a rotating cast of musicians playing for twenty-four hours, for instance—you can rest assured that a given performance of improvised music isn't going to last more than about an hour and a half. So, deep psychological trepidation (and fear of kitchen burners left alight) aside, there's nothing really so fretful about it. You can always leave if you're not enjoying it. That's an option. You are not trapped. I've left concerts I was really digging. Sometimes it's just the right thing to do. Maybe you've got an early morning or you're with someone who isn't having a good time or you've had enough to chew on already and feel musically sated. The first time I saw a retrospective of Willem de Kooning, I looked at three paintings and then left. More would have felt like gluttony. If you're done, *get out of there*. Don't hang around. There's nothing medicinal about listening to music you're not enjoying. It's not cod-liver oil. Enduring it will not make you a better person.

So keep in mind, you are in the driver's seat. That should help with some of the duration dread. And maybe such knowledge will help you relax and let yourself become immersed in the quite separate time domain of the music. That, to me, is the ideal way to listen. If the duration wigs you out, try not to come with anything else to do, nothing that will make you concerned about when the session will end. At least early on, don't bring friends who are negative about or highly skeptical of the music; that kind of energy can completely destroy your ability to pay attention and not worry about the duration. If you arrive clean, with an open schedule, ready to give it up to the music's new temporality, you'll be in good shape to pay attention and dig in.

Basic Identification: Who Is Doing What?

Thus far, our book's been on the defensive, overcoming obstacles and learning to let go of certain expectations. Fair enough, there's some baggage to unload. Now let's get on the good foot and start to elucidate positive things that you can watch for and pay attention to.

Whether you're watching birds or listening to music, any interpretive activity has three main ingredients: observation, comparison, and analysis. These are sequential, cumulative, and mandatory, meaning that you can't skip a step. And the first of them, observation, is the most important. Without keen observation, you'll get nowhere; you won't be able to fruitfully compare and therefore your analyses won't hold water. It's challenging—there are many distractions, other things vying for your attention—but if you don't focus, your interpretations will lack foundation.

If you go to a concert, you have the delightful advantage of being able to see the musicians as they play. This will help in the process of identifying them, singling out who is playing and what they're playing. It may sound rudimentary—well, in truth, it *is* rudimentary—but figuring out who's doing what is an essential first step in figuring out what's going on. If you can't identify the source, you'll have a tough time making heads or tails of how it gets combined with other sounds.

Think of a dish you really love. The overall experience is one thing, the flavor gestalt, but this quickly yields to more detailed reflection. "What's that spice?" you ask. "How did it get that texture? Is that a bit of tooth, or is it very crunchy?" You're trying to parse what's in your mouth, the first step in deciding whether it should stay there. "Is that sea urchin?" Out it comes, into the napkin.

I've been at concerts where I've spent the entire time trying and failing to figure out where one sound was coming from. It's not always as self-evident as it seems. Seeing the performers is a good clue, but it is by no means fail-safe. Someone who looks like they're doing nothing might be making a hellish racket, and someone gesticulating wildly might not be doing anything at all. With people playing laptops, it's especially confusing. "Is he making all those insane high-pitched pulsations, or is he checking his e-mail? Or both?" Who's to say, unless you happen to be seated right behind the guy.

The first order of business is to try to associate the agents with their actions, and viewing them is a pretty good guide. If you're not familiar with the kinds of sounds that various instruments can make, that's okay because many improvisors actually make sounds that are uncharacteristic of their instruments—or *were* uncharacteristic until they were discovered, lassoed, wrangled, and branded by the player. The term for this, which will be discussed later, is "extended techniques," and it's not exclusive to improvised music at all, but has been an important feature over the music's rather compact run.

An exercise might be helpful in learning to focus on who's doing what. Say you're at a concert featuring a quintet. Close your eyes and spend a little while listening to the whole thing, not worried about the parts. Get the gist of the composite sound. Now open up and focus your attention on a single player. Fix on that person for a bit. One by one, shift from one player to another and to yet another. Try to blank the others out, as if each were playing alone. Make the rounds a few times, and then when you feel comfortable with that, pretty sure you can recognize the sound of each of the participants, connect the dots, and shift your focus again to the five together.

The ability to do this, incidentally, has been given a wonderful technical name. It's called the Cocktail Party Effect.* Imagine you're at a fun and boisterous gathering, with people around a table

---

*This is specifically applied to speech recognition; the broader field of study is known as Auditory Scene Analysis.

talking to one another. They're actors. And they've been drinking. Tipsy theater people—the loudest kind! There's noise spilling out into the living room. You, from your vantage on the couch, can choose what part of the din you want to attend, which "stream" you would prefer to hear. Our listening is selective. And while you can do this without thinking, it's pretty miraculous. Humans are able to block out sounds and highlight other sounds, mentally, like a filmmaker using a close-up or a zoom. All the vibrations still get inside our ears and rattle the drums, but another function allows us to sort through them just after they land. Our brains are ridiculously good at recognition. And suppression.

These are the power tools of musician identification. Rely on your party-honed skills at recognizing and suppressing sound, and put them to good use figuring out what kind of mischief each of the players is up to.

Entrances and Exits: Mapping the Flow of Events

Building on the basic ID exercise, it's possible to move to the next level and begin to think a little more globally about a given performance. You'll need to be able to do this in order to understand not only about what's going on at any given moment, but how the improvisation is changing over its course—which calls for another exercise. This time, it's a mapmaking game, ultra-simple, unelaborated, and useful in beginning to comprehend how a piece of improvised music works.

Take out your notebook before a piece commences. From the time it starts until it's finished, in whatever shorthand or graphic notation you choose, jot down all of the entrances and exits

of the various musicians. When the saxophonist starts to do anything, note it; when the violin-
ist falls silent, note it. You can write it down it as
a list or, as I prefer, work horizontally, from left to
right, drawing lines that represent the presence of
each of the instruments. If you can, indicate the
length of time between changes proportionally, so
that longer stretches of an instrument playing are
plotted farther along on a continuum than brief
intrusions. If someone is playing intermittently,
note that, perhaps with a dotted line.

This is not a particularly pleasurable way to listen. Remind yourself: you're doing research. And
you're teaching yourself another way to pay attention. Depending on the performers and how they
are playing, you might not be able to keep up with
all the starting and stopping, entering and exiting.
Or you might find that everyone plays all the time,
never stops for a second.

Each time an improvisor starts or stops, they
have made a choice, a decisive move, clear and easy
to follow. Not all aspects of improvising are like
this; some decisions are quite hard to plumb. Here,
implicitly, we are touching base with the question

"Why?" Up until now, everything has been strict observation and reportage, but if someone chooses to stop or to enter, they're making a decision, and it's reasonable to ponder what has prompted that move. Did they decide that the music needed to thin out? Did they feel they had the perfect thing to add? Were they inspired by what one of the others had just done? Did they feel weird having already sat out so long and were compelled to jump back in out of guilt?

The whys of improvising are juicy stuff. It's worth contemplating motivation, but there's more basic material to master before getting too deep into such speculations.

What to do with your masterpiece once it's done? Frame it up? Enter it in a contest? Fold it and put it in the glove box with all the other maps? Actually I tricked you. It's not about the finished product—it's about the process and what this on-the-fly cartography forces you to do, the observations it allows you to make. It's a learning exercise. Your takeaway isn't just a marked-up sheet of paper; it's a revamped set of synapses. Sorry. It was for your own good.

Interaction Dynamics: The Core

Aside from soloists and electronic music, most kinds of live music rely on human interaction, the malleable, shifting nature of which makes it an intrinsic musical dynamic. It's part of what makes a great band better than an OK one. Lindsey Buckingham leans into a guitar solo, and Mick Fleetwood gooses the drums—they feel it, look at each other, and smile. But whereas in other kinds of music it manifests in nuanced detail, in improvised music interaction dynamics is the core.

The Car

A car is driving down the street. A handsome one, bright, with white racing stripes. A foreign model;

it's a few years old but still pristine. You admire it, take for granted how effortlessly it rolls along under its own steam; you adore its aerodynamics, the faux-leather interior, the pop-up headlights, the way it purrs. It's an entity, an immaculate machine. But under that fetching hood, there are hundreds of little mechanisms, all doing their own thing, linked up to one another, calibrated to make the car stop and go. The mechanisms have complex relationships. They signal one another, turn one another on and off, heat up, cool down, spark, explode, contain and concentrate energy, regulate speed and intensity and flow. They exist individually, apart, but engaged in a complex system. The separate parts conspire to give the overall impression of a single functional automobile.

Sit up straight. Look smart. Pay attention. This is the most important section of the book or, as my father-in-law says, the tastiest part of the pig.

Free improvisors tend to avoid or reject certain standard elements of the musical tool kit—steady rhythm, conventional harmony, melody. In the place of these usual objects of fascination, there's this other thing to pay attention to: interaction dynamics. How are the players relating to one another? What kinds of exchange are going on? Or not? Are they listening to the others, or are they off playing on their own? How does what they do correspond to the actions of the others?

Individual improvisors might be likened to the parts of that car: separate but interrelated. This is the single most exciting thing in the music, what sets it furthest apart from other kinds of music making, so you should perk up and learn what to listen for. The question is does the car metaphor hold?

At once the most visceral and the headiest aspect of improvised music, interaction dynamics might well be what you see when you look under the hood. All the idealism that is sometimes mapped on to free music—the notion that it's like a miniature model of egalitarian society; that it represents a communal way of working together—is extrapolated from the way players interact. The palpable sense of give-and-take and the excitement of watching musicians building something jointly are focal points for the inscrutable interaction-dynamics diagnostician.

Interaction dynamics are presupposed in many other kinds of music. This is true in large part because the various instruments tend to have prescribed roles. The drummer keeps time and pushes things along. The bassist helps with timekeeping and lays down a basic harmonic framework, elaborated upon by piano or guitar. Linear instruments like saxophones and trumpets and vocals and sitars tend to deal with melodies, most often played in the keys laid down by the harmony instruments. The relationships are like those between the carburetor and drive shaft and sparkplug—all organized in a known way so that the motor can move the chassis and the driver can count on the car doing its thing.

Not the Car

In improvised music, all those presuppositions go out the window.

When jazz drummers introduced the option of playing without pulsed time, for instance, they didn't just do so to be contrary or unorthodox or to make music that was difficult to listen to. They called their prescribed instrumental role into question. The drummers—specifically, it was Milford Graves, Sunny Murray, and Rashied Ali—wanted to open the music up in order to let some new things develop, and they realized that the conventional instrumental roles were an impediment to possible new directions. Pretty soon all the instruments were asking that same question: What is my supposed role, and what if I don't want to live by it?

If you want to hear one of the most radical moments in this alternative way of thinking, listen to the Albert Ayler Trio's *Spiritual Unity*, which was recorded over fifty years ago. The saxophone and bass and drums are doing something quite different from what they normally do—the bassist (Gary Peacock) is melodic, skittish, and virtuosic; the drummer (Sunny Murray) gathers pools and eddies of sound, mounting and dissipating volume, his cymbals awash in nervous energy; the saxophonist (Ayler) only plays a smidge of melodic material, concentrating on ecstatic shouts and cries, swooping across the others in big slurs and swipes, lightning flashing across a turbulent sea. The conventional roles of the instruments are upended, reinvented.

To return to the car metaphor, it would be like driving an automobile in which the relationships between the parts of the motor are repeatedly re-invented. All those hoses and fans and gears constantly reconnected, retooled, recalibrated. En route. The sparkplug suddenly not sparking, instead deciding to channel antifreeze. Perhaps not the most efficient motor vehicle. When it breaks down it's a disaster, but when it's humming along, like it was in the Ayler Trio's case, it sure is a fine ride. Rather unlike a car, in fact, it could be a vehicle created by Jean Tinguely, the metal sculptor whose kinetic machines took themselves apart as they whizzed and banged along. The relationship between the parts is different when the show is over than they are when it starts. Interaction dynamics? Hey, now: dynamic interactions.

Before we detail any of these interaction dynamics, first an overarching observational schema. In relation to what the others are doing, what each musician is contributing can be characterized as either (1) matching, (2) complementary, or (3) contrasting. The overall energy of the music might be said to be (1) concentrated or (2) diffused.

There are many different kinds of interaction dynamics. A few of the most common species follow here, enumerated and slightly elaborated, for your dining and dancing pleasure.

1. Dialogue

The easiest kind of interaction to recognize is the conversation. Just to keep it simple, take a duet. One player suggests something, the other responds and offers a bit more, the first one builds on the response, and so on. Carried out too obviously, dialogue can turn into a musical seesaw, one up/ one down, not really going anywhere or developing. But it's elemental, an essential part of musical communication. As in daily life, when you hear people exchanging ideas this way, it tells you one key thing: they're listening to one another, paying attention to what the other is saying. That conveys a certain kind of respect and dignity, and when it's really working, it can have an organic quality, rolling effortlessly like a late-night bull session. Also, adding more players makes dialogue exponentially more complex and difficult. Like a round-table discussion, dialogical improvising has an upper threshold of participants. Anything good with more than six players is pretty unusual. (Or it requires a moderator, like a musical score or a conductor.) A really good, really big free improvising group, like a ten-piece, is nearly mythological.

2. Independent Simultaneous Action

Picture two old folks in a room, a George Booth cartoon: a woman, standing at the ironing board, chattering about her garden; her husband, chest deep in a bathtub, cigar stub in mouth, newspaper open, furrowed brow; two dogs and a cat scattered around the space, each looking a different direction, every sight line going its own way like a demagnetized compass. Together alone.

On the other end of the spectrum from direct

dialogue, there are improvisations in which the participants don't seem to pay much attention to one another at all. On the face of it, this seems disastrous, counterintuitive; but it can lead to some wonderful music and is often an important ingredient in the overall fabric of an improvisation because it introduces tension and takes away the Ping-Pong-ness of conversational interplay.

Saxophonist Evan Parker, an uncommonly articulate commentator, has suggested that improvisations fall into those that express agreement, those that express disagreement, and those in which the participants agree to disagree. Independent simultaneous action calls up this last category, in which there isn't direct conflict but there's also no sense of concertedness. Two (or more) players in a space do their own thing, the result being a sonic collage of separate activities, an overlay of sounds.

Most improvisors who practice this kind of non-interplay are quite aware of what the other musicians are doing. Players cultivate peripheral hearing; they train themselves to listen out of the corner of their ears. It takes this studied sort of indifference to continue doing your own thing when someone else has made a bold, attention-grabbing statement. And even when players are working together, if one breaks off and starts down a new path, a possible strategy is for the other player not to change course, but to continue as if they were still working jointly, staying on the same path. Take a saxophonist and a drummer, Peter Brötzmann and Han Bennink, for instance, bringing things to a boil, playing hot-and-heavy energy music—all of a sudden, paddling the snare with a mighty whack, Bennink slams on the brakes. If Brötzmann continues apace, his tenor sax ferociously barreling along, this has an inherent dramatic effect, like Wile E. Coyote running out of cliff. In this case, you can imagine how the musicians must be palpably aware of their own momentum and the momentum of the total music at the same time. That ability to hear the specific and the general at once is basic to improvising. The musicians have to work together and be prepared to stand apart more or less at any instant.

Improvisation is social music. The shapes it

takes and the methods used to make it are collective in nature, often gregarious, interactional. Like the inner workings of a pride of lions, a parliament of owls, a cloud of bats, a bloat of hippos. But there are antisocial elements in the music, too, solitary, uncommunicative moments, times when the collective is shunned in favor of the individual. The antisocial impulse helps keep the music from growing predictable. Just like our beloved introverts and eccentrics do in daily life.

Let's say the two extremes are complete dependence and absolute independence. Players either slavishly rely on one another or pay absolutely no mind to anyone else whatsoever. In between there's a gray area, where most of the activity really occurs: interdependence. Improvisors are constantly modulating these interaction dynamics in subtle ways, moving along that scale, by turns listening to and willfully ignoring one another. As a listener, the challenge in the case of independence is to hear the composite, to feel the buildup of tension—or perhaps to experience the dissipation of tension—of two or more colliding bodies, each self-contained. There's no guarantee that a passage of independent simultaneous action won't go awry and end up a pile of unrelated sounds. But neither is there any assurance that interdependence will work—it's all a nest of contingencies, different strategies that improvisors use, mostly by intuition, to navigate the unknown.

3. Imitation

Have you ever met someone with echolalia? Someone who repeats everything you say right after you've said it? A little audio shadow, like those slap-back phone echoes you sometimes get on transatlantic calls? The doubled words—hello *hello*, Mom *Mom*, can you *can you* hear me *hear* meeeee?—get tangled, making discourse awkward and stilted. For those afflicted, echolalia is a genuine malady. In improvised music, rote imitation is an extreme interaction dynamic that can be effective in rare instances but is often a mark of younger and more inexperienced players. It's easy to spot. One person plays a high, pinched note, chirping like a car alarm, another continues the same sound on a different instrument. Or the drummer plays a pattern, and the cellist picks it up and repeats it. Imitation is a clear way for one player to indicate to another: *I'm listening to you!* But it can just as easily feel like *I can do that too!* Or it can take on an air of parody or ridicule: *Oh, look what* we're *doing now!*

This is the most brutal and obvious version of imitation. There are many ways in which improvisors pick up on and vary the material that their colleagues put on the table. Listen for those places where one player suggests an idea—a particularly tone or sequence, a rhythmic pattern, an unusual sound quality—and another follows and develops it. That's one of the most vital areas in free improvised music, the place where sounds are jointly pushed and pulled. But the best players know to proceed cautiously as far as mynah-birding is concerned.

4. Consensus/Dispute

Improvised music is not, by any means, all warm and fuzzy. There's the agree-to-disagree posse, independent simultaneity, but then there's also just plain disagreement. In the context of improvising, an unusually high level of disagreement between participants is possible. I'd argue that this is one of its unique features. People playing together don't even need to concur in principle on what it means to improvise. In fact, there's quite a lot of variance on that point, players coming not only from very different traditions but also from very different personal points of view, expressing and engaging philosophies of improvising that are not only different but at odds.

This makes for excellent listening, just the way you could imagine it would make for wonderful people-watching. Paying attention to the various ways that consensus and dispute manifest in a given performance is akin to being on a train and listening to folks in the next row snuggle or argue. There's something electromagnetically fascinating about it.

Dispute can come from a source of underlying philosophical disharmony—two players duking it out on behalf of different standpoints. But more often it's a matter of a musician feeling a need emerge in the music for a little contrary energy, something to allow one, as a senior improvisor once told me, not to swim with the school but to *bite at the feet of the others.*

There's a flow. Things are moving along. This is a normal thing in improvising. The music is going in a direction, pulling all together and forward. But maybe someone pushes against the flow, either diverting it or impeding it. This is a form of subversion. And it can work by many means, not just flailing against the tide. Guitarist Derek Bailey provided a detailed description of the way that Hugh Davies once used his electronics to perversely protract something that Evan Parker was doing beyond its logical endpoint. Just at the point of Parker's running out of breath, Davies started playing along with him, dialoguing with him, forcing Parker to either artificially interrupt the music or to continue at the expense of great personal exhaustion. It would have been like someone starting a conversation and the partner not responding a few parries in. Ever the gentleman, Parker struggled to continue, which probably gave the performance a special kind of character: a fragile, almost-falling-apart feeling.

Improvisors can be imps. They like to get a rise out of one another, to nip at the heels, jostle, and cajole. They also like to build things, to work together on a common cause. But working together doesn't mean all doing the same thing. It's not synchronized swimming. Watch for the impish moments, the places where someone makes an abrasive or contrary move. And keep an ear out for the consensual moments, where you have the overall feeling everyone's on the same page, the troops are rallied, the wagons are packed, and the caravan hits the road.

A final consideration: at times dispute in improvising is left unresolved because it betrays what one experienced figure refers to as "a misunderstanding." That is, the parties involved can't find a way to work together, and despite wanting to, they can't find a joint solution. This kind of kludge makes for very uncomfortable listening, like when you hear people trying to have a conversation but not able to connect.

5. Support/Stepping Up

The questioning of conventional roles doesn't mean improvisors can't adopt roles ad hoc as the music proceeds. For example, within the "building together" modality, something that often takes place is a process of stepping up. And when someone steps up, unless they decide to square off and tussle, the others usually need to find something to do to support the stepper-upper.

There are countless versions of this, but it's pretty fundamental. In jazz it would simply be referred to as a solo, but in freely improvised music it's often a bit more subtle—one player is foregrounded, takes it upon themselves to make a statement, and the others back off or find some kind of platform for the statement. That platform could be a low drone or a repeated figure or just dropping out and letting the player step up unaccompanied.

I've seen the saxophonist Ken Vandermark employ this strategy quite a lot, particularly on pieces where he's playing clarinet. Out of a complex, multifaceted passage featuring lots of dense interplay, Vandermark might step up and lay a definitive melodic clarinet statement over whatever else his compatriots are doing. This has a narrative, storytelling quality, as if, out of the abstract bramble, there was a tale yearning to be spun. Vandermark's pretty masterful at peddling the story and managing not to assume a controlling position, a selfish move that makes everyone else subservient and can kill forward impetus as fast as a blowout on the highway.

6. Making Space vs. Being Tentative

Someone who steps up all the time might not be leaving enough room for anyone else. This is another observable phenomenon: the activity of making space. If someone's playing is so busy that it's impenetrable, that can make it difficult for anyone else to find a way into the music. It's like someone who never stops talking—this takes the "inter" out of "interaction." All kinds of narcissism and personality disorders come to the fore in improvised music—it's such a profoundly social music, that it's almost like you could use it to make a psychological profile of the participants. But it's an art form, too, not just a window on the musi-cians' psyches; and top-flight players use these dy-namics to their own ends, sometimes adopting a persona that's different from the one they have in everyday life. Shy ones become animals; monsters become wallflowers.

An otherwise friendly player might "crowd" the others to get a specific result, to force them to step up, for instance, or to draw out some kind of latent aspect of their playing. On the other hand, when players make space for one another, there's a threshold after which the act can express a ten-tativeness, overpoliteness, sometimes with dis-astrous results. Suddenly everyone's saying: "No, after *you*." Improvised music is like a balloon, it needs some tension to keep it taut; lose the ten-sion, and the music farts around and falls limp on the floor.

7. Counterpoint

Listening to an improvisation, I sometimes hear the sounds in terms of dance. Here, the dancers are not all doing the same thing—again, it's not synchronized swimming. But they're working together, notes dovetailing, the music assembling and disassembling like a couple doing the tango, energies conspiring, one moving forward, the other backward—a stop, a spin, and back together. The notion of counterpoint helps. Introduced during the Renaissance, developed in baroque music, and explored extensively by J. S. Bach, counterpoint has to do with the idea that you can have two (or more) simultaneous melodies that are perceived as independent lines and at the same time maintain a harmonic relationship. Remember "Row, Row, Row Your Boat"? A canon. That's an ultra-simple form of counterpoint.

I have a fond memory of seeing saxophonist John Zorn and cornetist Butch Morris play together. Their interplay was incredibly intimate, featuring tiny little sounds and contrasting loud outbursts. All very oblique, played at high speed, changing rapidly. You could listen to each of them as an entity, an unassailable identity, but there was also clear communication, and what they were doing fit snugly together. This is called free counterpoint, meaning that it doesn't adhere to the harmonic requirements of so-called "strict" counterpoint. At any given moment, Zorn and Morris didn't have to be playing according to a sequence of chord changes. They were entities, identities, unique and apart, but they folded these identities together, tumbling them like rocks in a polisher, the friction of the two identities together creating shiny new ones.

Togetherness and independence: these are basic genomes of interaction dynamics in improvisation. At times one or the other of them rises to the top, but much of the time it's a matter of being able to listen to the activity with both in mind. In the combo platter of contrapuntal improvising, togetherness and independence find their apotheosis.

Dynamics Dynamics: Passive-Aggressive Improvising

There are interaction dynamics, and there are just plain dynamics.

In any kind of music, dynamics is a technical term that covers the range of possible volumes at which particular sound might be made, from *pianissimo* (very quiet) to *fortissimo* (very loud). In listening to improvisation, it's a valuable tool to be attentive to dynamics. They can tell you a great deal about what's going on, and watching skilled improvisors handle subtleties of volume is a special treat.

Manipulating dynamics is incredibly challenging, and younger improvisors often inadvertently play at the same dynamic level all the time. They do this because they're too caught up in trying to improvise to be aware of the flow of the overall picture, the way that thickening up or thinning out a passage just by varying volume can be so crazily effective.

Here's another exercise: attend a concert with the intention of simply listening for volume shifts. Do the musicians have a tendency to go in one direction all the time? Are the dynamics complex and varied, or do they conform to one kind of profile? Is there a pattern you can discern in the rise and dip of loudness?

One common contour that improvisations—particularly epic ones lasting more than an hour—tend to take is that of peaks and valleys. Think of a landscape excerpted from the world of Pippi Longstocking: dizzying mountains with snow-capped tops and peaceful canyons with flowing streams and plains of short grass. Now make a silhouette line drawing of it, and imagine music that fits the shape. At the highest point, the musicians are yodeling at the top of their lungs, rattling teeth; down below, they're whispering willows, barely audible. Over the course of the concert, back and forth, the music climbs to the peaks and descends to the valleys, stopping to milk a goat or nap on an outcropping along the way.

Sometimes improvisors use dynamics to control events. Loudness is a powerful tool in this regard. The most common version has to do with a certain kind of energy: the stark-raving mad screamer. Sometimes a languid improvisation needs some defibrillation to get the blood flowing again. An innards-curdling holler can prove just the electric paddle for the job. They say the squeaky wheel gets the grease, and sometimes it's true that the loudest improvisor gets the most attention and dictates events. Forceful interplay, with players jousting violently for position, can be good, cathartic, medieval fun, though it can also be tiresome for the audience and merely calisthenic for the players. Some of the figures known for being loud, in truth, have a very soft and sensitive side— theirs is a romantic streak, whatever the volume. Peter Brötzmann is an excellent example, his more delicate music often unjustly overshadowed by his reputation as a blowhard.

There's another kind of power broker in improvising who is a bit harder to spot but still well worth watching out for: the low talker. We all know them in everyday life, people who speak very softly in order to make you pay attention. You have to move in close, stop breathing, assume a meditative stance, and concentrate hard just to hear what they're murmuring. Low talking is a form of control. In the right hands, it can be as aggressive as a vuvuzela blown through a megaphone.

Super-low dynamics is a specialty in some camps. In its jazz prehistory, it was wielded successfully by Jimmy Giuffre, whose beautiful *sotto voce* clarinet playing has undeniable force and finesse. A recent splinter group of improvisors, largely under the influence of trombonist Radu Malfatti, gave name to the art of low-speaking free music, calling it "lowercase" improvising. The handle is almost as precious and passive-aggressive as the music itself.

Quiet can come as a relief, but just as easily it can be oppressive. It can feel natural or mannered, depending on how it's wielded. Personally, I'm a fan of low-dynamics/tiny-little-sounds improvising when it still has some juice. It is best heard in situations with no need for amplification, where the acoustics of the room and the interplay between participants rather than the will of a sound-man dictate what can be heard, what can't, and what teeters on the edge.

One thing that I've grown very tired of is something I've observed in certain low-dynamics situations, what you could call the politics of volume shame. Some members of the quietude club dictate an overall intolerance of loudness or energy or interruption, manipulated by means of stern looks and a pompous, self-serious, hushed breathlessness. Nothing should break the magical spell. Tedious. Boring. The wrong kind of attitude for an improvisor.

Transitions:
Observing How
the Music Changes

I once engineered a studio recording for three string players, cellist Fred Lonberg-Holm and bassists Kent Kessler and Peter Kowald. Kowald, the elder statesman of the threesome, proposed a particular strategy for some of the pieces: they should do a suite of short improvisations based on the idea that as soon as the music felt like it was about to change, rather than following the impulse, they would stop. Hearing them do this was incredibly instructive for me as a listener. It made me acutely aware of the transition points in the music, places where something that had developed and stabilized would be left behind and something different would take over.

In physics, they call these phase transitions. Like when a substance goes from solid to liquid or from liquid to gas. It's about moving from one steady state to another. Sometimes in improvised music there's enough disparate stuff going on that it's hard to hear the steady states. The constant change gives it a perpetual feeling, like when Fibber McGee opens the closet and unleashes an endless clattering of junk. When the music refuses to settle in, it can introduce a pleasant kind of vertigo that makes my stomach flutter.

The contemporary classical composer Karlheinz Stockhausen had a name for this sensibility, a sort of idealized eternal present: moment form. According to this approach, a given musical event should feel neither like it came out of anything before it nor should it suggest a direction that it's headed. It should just be what it is: discrete, a moment, an intensity, crystallized and then let go, followed by another unique moment, apprehended and released. No chain of events. No development. No past. No future.

Listening to moment-form improvising is like

surfing. You have to get on the wave and ride, let the tidal motion carry you forward, but be prepared for the froth of change when the wave breaks. But not many improvisations manage to hold on to moment form. That, in part, is because people's memories intervene, keeping the immediate past suspended in their minds as current events gush ever onward. Again, as one discovers in many circumstances listening to the music, free improvisation has something in common with meditation. Thoughts come into view, are perceived, and the attempt is made to let go of them. But it's only the true masters who can go thoughtless, making their minds into blank slates on to which the present is projected, outside of time's bow and arrow.

When the surf is low and Om is scarce, improvisations tend to move in sequence through steady states, each one being invented and explored on the spot and, once exhausted, abandoned for the next plateau. As a listener, it can be edifying to look for those transition points, identifying the places where one kind of sound-making gives way to another. Try to find the exact temperature at which the ice melts or the water evaporates. This is a little more advanced, but it's still elemental. If you can start to feel the way an improvisation is shifting, the nodes of change and the passages of stasis, you naturally start to hear the piece as a whole, which is essential if you want to assess anything about the broader implications of its shape and structure.

Structure:
The Butcher Shop

So let's say you're adept at all the basics so far. You're cool with the lack of preplanned rhythmic design; you're comfortable with open-ended duration. You easily identify who's doing what and when. You're keyed in on the various species of interaction, effortlessly follow variations in dynamics, and take note of transition points as the music unfolds. And it feels perfectly natural attending to all of this in real time.

It could be time to try applying these to a bigger project: evaluating structure. By this, I mean understanding how the parts—individual moments, or the steady states that transitions bridge—fit together, how they are structured. And, in turn, how they relate to the whole. Think of those butcher shop posters, with an animal mapped out into segments; to understand a particular cut, you've got to have a picture of where it fits on the beast.

This will be tremendously variable. For the players and the listener alike, structure is highly dependent on memory. It pushes at the limits of brainpower, forces the issue of the music's ephemeral existence, its unrepeatability. Recordings may help, but, really, they're a different kind of phenomenon—like a photograph of a party, they don't say much about the actual feeling, the atmosphere, the context. We'll delve into the phenomenology of recorded improvisations later, but for our purposes now, listening for structural implications of live improvised music is the name of the game.

I'm going to spell out two general kinds of structure, leaving it for you to ID and tag others. This should help get you started. First, and most conventional, is a structure that builds toward an endpoint. All the different segments, whether long or short or vastly or faintly different, accumulate in a manner that seems directed, aimed at a finale, a climax, if you will. Improvised music can adopt this classical narrative structure, complete with introduction, exposition, conflict, and resolution.

The play of parts in this schema happens according to a mounting logic. Let's say the dynamics start softly; they might gradually build until there's a mighty conflict and then die back down partially as a signal for the dénouement. Meanwhile, the overall speed of the music might pick up, again suggesting mounting energy, and more of the players might be playing more of the time later in the piece, making it denser, heavier, cumulative. This is a particular arc, a dramatic one, common to other kinds of narrative music, such as Western classical music of the Romantic era. Most of the time, the diverse sections point forward, any contrary motion added simply to thicken the plot. It is a cathartic structure.

In contrast, almost diametrically opposed to this dramatic structure is one that features juxtaposition. Here the logic is not mounting; it refrains from building tension—instead it holds interest by means of contrast. A loud section is followed by a soft one, followed by one that is medium loud, followed by a loud one. A spiky section is followed by a smooth one, juxtaposed with one featuring lots of wavy motion. Parts are held up against one another, the point being not having a point.

Of course, we live in a goal-oriented world, where undirected activity is considered a waste of time. To get what's going on in this kind of improvising, you have to let go of that idea and embrace a non-narrative, nonlinear sensibility. When you feel the music moving in this way, you should try to imagine the various musical elements as objects. Watch the musicians move them around on the table, take some away, put new ones into the mix. The frame of the table stays the same, the objects are static, the relationship of the elements changes. It's more like a chemistry experiment than a short story.

This is part of the retarded legacy of contemporary classical music in free improvisation. And I mean retarded literally—it's about being stuck, static, not propelled forward, but staying in one place. It's often cast as being archetypically European, as opposed to the narrative, propulsive legacy of African American music. That's too reductive a dichotomy to hold water for long; within the jazz tradition, there are foreshadowings of this way of working, in Thelonious Monk's circumspect solos, for instance, or the perfectly illogical logic of some of Sonny Rollins's solos. But as a simplified way of talking about it, maybe it's a little helpful.

Discerning structure is a major challenge for the fledgling listener. It requires paying attention to what's going on in a given moment at the same time as considering the thing as a whole. This entails the mental act of remembering and reconstructing, putting all the pieces back together retrospectively, and cogitating over their relationships. And bear in mind, if the music was freely improvised, there was no advance plan, no preliminary sketch. The structure was decided on the spot. The musicians didn't have to adhere to a particular organizational scheme. So you are trying to discern a structure that the musicians themselves might not actually identify, one they may not have expected, one that unfolded organically, as an expression of shared time and effort.

Imagine a construction site, all dust and dirt and flapping plastic. This building has no blueprint. It is built brick upon brick, wall to wall, floor by floor, as the materialization of a fantasy held jointly by multiple architects working with masons and carpenters at the same instant on the same edifice. If this were actually a building, it would probably be a mess; it would certainly be dangerous, structurally unsound. Fortunately, in improvised music, it's not a concrete structure that's being erected. It doesn't have to be structurally sound for sound to have a structure.

Personal Vocabulary: Each unto Themselves

From the global to the subatomic—now we pull focus and zoom in on the smallest particle of the music, which adheres to the individual player: personal vocabulary. Technically this will be the end of the fundamentals and the beginning of a more advanced approach to our fieldwork. While all the rest of the basics of listening to improvised music that we have discussed are possible without knowing really anything about the cast of characters and their history, with this concept it's helpful to build up a repository of information about specific players, what they do, their performance vitae, the bands they have worked with, any details that come to hand. And you might have to know something about how various instruments are played, at least enough to understand what's different about the way someone blows or scrapes or bows or whacks.

Each player amasses a range of techniques and sensibilities that can be described as a sort of lexicon. It's not that these are fixed—indeed, in concert there is sometimes such a heightened environment that new inflections are discovered on the spot. But the things that a musician practices and develops, the sounds they use in the course of playing with others, these are their personal vocabulary; if they are not part of the conventional inventory of things to do on a given instrument, they are often referred to as "extended techniques." The seasoned listener recognizes them and, moreover, can hear when they have been deployed in an especially wonderful or novel way. The context of others should optimally challenge players to expand or flex their lexicon. The personal vocabulary can't be rote like punching the keys of a Speak & Spell, although there are such improvisors: dreadful, non-listening show-offs who demon-

strate their special skills rather than actually playing music. In the best hands, the personal vocab
expresses its pliability; rigid materials are hard to
work with, largely avoided in favor of those that
can be easily manipulated.

Rather than concentrate on the interactive,
from this perspective we watch for things that set
each player apart, the characteristics of their playing, with special attention to their signature moves.
A few players have consciously tried to avoid this,
people whose approach is exclusively interactive
and who have decided not to develop a personal
vocabulary but instead utilize a rather standard
set of materials and techniques. This most often
is prompted by a political inclination, a wariness
of overemphasizing individualism. I will admit
my prejudice against this kind of music. It's noble
in theory, but in practice it's dull. It tends to produce a generalized sound, predictable and average;
it leads to what we might call lumpen improvising.

Evan Parker once described the Dutch improvised music scene as being invested in remarkable
personalities, meaning there's an amplification

or intensification of personal identity amongst those players. "The Dutch are not much interested in what Misha [Mengelberg] calls mood music, which is music where the musician becomes lost in the process, transported into what I understand is for Misha a grotesque, trancelike state, where all rational decision-making gets lost, and the idea becomes less important than the experience."* The "remarkable personalities" approach is perhaps extra-true of the Amsterdam scene, with outsize characters like Misha, Han Bennink, and Willem Breuker; but it's an aspect of all the best improvisors, too, no matter where they come from. Trombonist Günter Christmann has explained that although you can find all sorts of weird and wacky sounds to make on any instrument, the job of the improvisor is to really deeply examine which of the potential squeaks, hisses, and rasps he or she feels connected to, and to develop a special vocabulary based on those sounds.

I think that a listener can follow a similar dic-

*Evan Parker, quoted in Kevin Whitehead, *New Dutch Swing* (New York: Billboard Books, 1998), p. 46.

tum, developing their own vocabulary of listening. Listen for all the different kinds of playing, and find those musicians whose way of playing connects with you. You may find yourself dazzled by someone who blows his clarinet mouthpiece through a long hose connected to a paper shredder—for a little while, that is. But the most spectacularly unusual, freaky vocabularies are not always the most interesting in the long term. There was an improvisor who, in a mercifully short career, exclusively played balloons—mostly rubbing a wet finger on them to make them bray and snort like a donkey. It was fascinating for a short stretch, but then it grew old and there was no way for her to vary it. And eventually listeners completely lost interest in it.

I remember hearing the guitarist Davey Williams for the first time and being entranced by the way he played. It had all the crunchy obstinacy of Derek Bailey that I adored but also bore a surreal sense of humor and an earthy dose of the blues. Williams was endlessly flexible and could roll with anything his comrades threw at him, sometimes going off on his own direction, sometimes engaging in rapid-fire banter. I had already studied the recordings of Bailey, so I had his music as a baseline, and soon I'd learn about Eugene Chadbourne, John Russell, Henry Kaiser, Fred Frith, and other free-improvising guitarists. I'd parse their personal vocabularies, comparing and contrasting elements of each lexicon. Start with one player. Then go deeper and it becomes a web, a net of names to be explored laterally, associatively, through their arsenal of sounds. That's how I suggest you build on your foundation as a listener: with the fundamentals under control, go explore the personal vocabularies of extraordinary personalities and the hairpin high jinks that ensue when they assemble and stretch out.

Advanced Techniques

On Watching
While Listening

The musicians are right there in front of you. That's convenient because you can watch what they're doing, helping you answer myriad questions as they arise. For some listeners, improvised music is really only something to care about in concert; it's about the experience of sharing the space and time with the players, watching how they do their thing, the social theater of seeing them work together, adding all their actions and interactions to the logbook of observations, then compounding that with aspects observed about the music itself. In some cases, the two become inseparable. Seeing is hearing with the eyes; hearing is seeing with the ears.

Of course, I love going to see improvised music in concert. Note I use the word "see" here in the general sense of "attend." Make no mistake: if you have not been to a concert of improvised music, you don't have the first idea of what's what. But I also think it's worth considering the relative merits of watching while listening. If you get too hooked on all the clues that seeing gives you, it might make your listening practices less acute. Hence, it's useful to deprive yourself of seeing the musicians now and then.

The composer and sound theorist Michel Chion has adopted a special term developed by the inventor of *musique concrète*, Pierre Schaeffer: "acousmatic." Chion reckons that, for a variety of understandable reasons, our first impulse when encountering new sounds is to try to place them, to pin them down by asking where they came from and what made them. He calls this the "sound hermeneutic." Unrecognized sounds beg questions (*What made that sound? Where does it originate from?*). Watching musicians automatically answers them. (*Oh, look, it's that hurdy-gurdy on the right side of the stage!*)

If you suspend those questions, instead trying to analyze the sounds on their own terms *as sounds*, rather than as signs of a particular instrument or musical idea, then you hear them acousmatically. It's like looking at a jungle and thinking of it as a set of shapes and colors and textures rather than as leaves and trunks and animals and flowers. And it can be more than a formal reduction, because it can relate to energies, movement, sequence. Acousmatic listening requires some specialized language and concepts—frequency, timbre, overtones, harmonics, register, cluster, consonance and dissonance, noise. But I also think you can do it without knowing about all that stuff. You can be a self-taught acousmatician.

The easiest way to listen acousmatically is with a record. By their nature, records sever the relationship between the seen and the heard, and this is one of the reasons I'm a great lover of improvised music in its recorded form. You can listen in acousmatic mode, holding at bay the urge to figure out who's doing what. Or you can treat it more as a sort of ongoing quiz, testing your ability to identify the musicians, either by their instruments or, if you know their music pretty well, by their personal vocabularies. Either way, it's likely to enhance your listenership, make your ears keener.

Even listening to live music, I sometimes close my eyes to concentrate more fully on the sounds and abandon the world of the optical. It's a very good way to concentrate. If you're not careful, and you're at all snoozy, it can also be a mighty fine way to doze off. But, assuming the music is good, it should captivate you, hold your attention, and keep that accidental catnap at bay.

Live or Memorex?

Six things improvised music records are not good for:

1. Fun at a dance party.
2. A backdrop for nookie.
3. Studying.
4. Dinner music.
5. Reliving a favorite concert.
6. Experiencing the open-endedness of improvisation.

Six things improvised music records are good for:

1. Clearing a dance party.
2. Attentive listening.

3. Headphones.
4. Analyzing passages via repetition.
5. Not being distracted by facial expressions.
6. Impressing other record collectors.

Kindling: 20 Starter Records for Your Improvised Music Collection

1. Paul Rutherford, *The Gentle Harm of the Bourgeoisie*
2. Joe McPhee, *Sonic Elements*
3. Peter Evans, *Nature/Culture*
4. Paul Lytton, *?!*
5. Derek Bailey/Min Xiao-Fen, *Viper*
6. Charlotte Hug and Fred Lonberg-Holm, *Fine Extensions*
7. Polly Bradfield/Eugene Chadbourne, *Torture Time*
8. Cecil Taylor & Tony Oxley, *Leaf Palm Hand*
9. Irène Schweizer/Louis Moholo, *Irène Schweizer/ Louis Moholo*
10. Anthony Braxton/Joe Morris, *Four Improvisations (Duo) 2007*

11. AMM, *The Inexhaustible Document*
12. Schlippenbach Trio, *Elf Bagatellen*
13. Peter Brötzmann/Fred Van Hove/Han Bennink, *Brötzmann/Van Hove/Bennink*
14. Günter Christmann/Paul Lovens/Maarten Altena, *Weavers*
15. Barry Guy/Mats Gustafsson/Raymond Strid, *Tarfala*
16. Günter Christmann/Torsten Müller/LaDonna Smith/Davey Williams, *White Earth Streak*
17. Evan Parker Electroacoustic Ensemble, *Hasselt*
18. London Improvisers Orchestra, *Improvisations for George Riste*
19. Peter Brötzmann/Chicago Tentet, *American Landscapes 1*
20. King Übü Örchestrü, *Binaurality*

Once vs. Ongoing

Getting deeper into freely improvised music, you'll begin to notice certain overall tendencies. One basic drift has to do with the kinds of relationship maintained—or abandoned—amongst the improvisors. Some tend to treat their performances like one-night stands—playing one time with people they've just met—while others are the musical version of monogamists. At first blush, this might seem to be an artifact of circumstance, based on who invites whom to play with them, but I think it's more concerted than that. Indeed, it takes some effort these days to hold together a group. For organizers of the music, it's always attractive to present something new, previously un-tried; hence, the call for an endless permutation of lineups in festivals and at regular performance venues. Once an ensemble has made the rounds a few times, it can be difficult to convince a venue to take them again, for fear that audiences won't come out. Having organized series and festivals myself, I can empathize with this impulse. And it can lead to interesting and fruitful new combina-tions—indeed, if you don't try some fresh combi-nations, you may leave some great music on the table. The desire for something different led Peter Brötzmann and me to invite the members of his Chicago Tentet to work together; they transformed what might have been a weekend of gigs into a de-cade as a band.

But, generally, novelty mongering is a bad habit. The assumption, we can infer, is that once you've seen a group a couple of times, you might not want to see them again because you think they'll be re-peating themselves. If they're good improvisors, that's the opposite of true. In fact, the more you hear a good ensemble play together, the better your experience will be. You'll begin to understand what's going on at a deeper level, not just on the surface. You'll grow as a listener specific to the group, and if they're genuine improvisors, you'll be hearing them challenge themselves to play something different from before, to get further into the DNA of their particular configuration.

In the olden days, fifty years ago, if you lived in New York, you could go to the Five Spot and catch Thelonious Monk with the same ensemble for weeks on end, and then at the same club you could hear the new kid on the block, Ornette Coleman, with his iconoclastic group, night after night for fifteen weeks straight. I went to see Von Freeman with the same group at the New Apartment Lounge in Chicago for a decade of Tuesdays. Going to a run of these concerts was like a pilgrimage. You were hearing history in the making, listening to a group evolve in real time, making its way from a one-cell organism into a bipedal creature. Not too many opportunities like this exist anymore, but if you make a point of it, you can look forward to hearing a group play repeatedly. Henry Threadgill and his band Zooid recently played a weeklong residency at the Village Vanguard; I wish I could have seen all seven nights.

At the heart of this is a distinction between players who like the experience of novelty—the "once" crew—and those who prefer to explore the music together in an ongoing way. We return to the notion of interaction dynamics. Think of first encounters with people you meet. They tend to be cordial, polite, guided by the protocols of genial intercourse. *Nice to meet you. I've heard so much about you.* And so on. In these cases, in spite of their cordiality, people are sometimes very demonstrative, showing who they are, perhaps boasting a bit, trying to come off in a good light. *Look, I've got this special thing I can do, isn't it cool?*

Watching initial meetings of players can certainly be amusing, especially if you like the individual participants. They can be volatile encounters, since there's not much common ground yet, and people may do weird things when they are first introduced. I've attended a few such concerts that have really surprised me, like Derek Bailey's duet with Cecil Taylor, in which the guitarist took an uncharacteristically supportive, rather than combative, role. But on the whole, I must admit that first encounters have less caloric content than those where the players have been working together over time.

A dating vs. marriage model is perhaps helpful. Newness is always appealing, the thrill of the unknown, hearing stories and seeing someone naked for the first time. But improvisors actually take more chances and build trust if they play together regularly, just the way that married folks have to keep the home fires burning by learning more about their partners, finding the unexpected in the context of vast shared experience. That's super exciting. When you hear musicians who share a core understanding but are willing to take chances with that compact, there's much more at stake, the interaction is more deeply dramatic, and the payoff is richer.

The great things in any kind of art are not just the biggest, most obvious gestures. It's all in the nuance. Subtle cues. In-jokes. A gesture with a slightly different inflection. The way a player initiates or responds to another player based on their deep repository of shared history. Confidences established, shaken, dismantled, rebuilt. The intimacy of shared history. For me, that's the money shot.

The Level of Mystery

Evan Parker gave me a little tutorial once that has proven one of the most helpful things I've learned about improvised music. I'll pass it along to you here.

It may be interesting for the listener to be able to see why everything happens; that the process be listenable has a use. But I think that what is even more interesting is when the process is lost and things happen that are clearly the basis for an understanding, but the understanding is no longer worked through at the overt, explicit level. That's an important qualitative transition in improvised music. You have improvised music where it's pretty clear what kinds of things can happen and why and when. And then you have improvised music where the fact there's an understanding is clear, but quite how it works is moved to a level of mystery again.

So, you take all you've learned in fundamentals, the skills of close observation, trying to decipher what kind of interactions are happening, the provocations and responses, the convergences and divergences, and you put them away for a minute and instead enjoy the wonder of something you can't quite grasp, something mysterious. Parker concluded that "the whole thing seems to be operating at a level that involves . . . certainly intuition, and maybe faculties of a more paranormal nature." His long-term comrade, bassist Barry Guy, once told me that he believed in hearing through his bones. Because sound travels as much as four times as fast in liquids and non-porous solids than in air, he insisted that he could sense the music immediately, long before it made its way through the convoluted path of the outer ear, drum, stirrups, cochlea, basilar membrane, organ of Corti, sensory hairs, auditory nerve, to the brain.

If you're paying attention that way, by means of other portals of hearing, maybe via some otherwise unavailable psychic wavelength, either as a player or as a member of the audience, this will of course present a challenge for more conventional kinds of listening. But it doesn't mean that all the prep was for naught. You'll only encounter the level of mystery now and then. Savor it. Sit back, relax, and admit that something's taking place that is beyond you. Sorry to be so metaphysical, but the correct response to the level of mystery is awe.

The Ambiguous and the Unresolved: Is Tony Dead?

I read in the *New York Times* about a burning issue of our day: is Tony Soprano alive or dead? *The Sopranos* ended in 2007. The last episode seems quite determined to leave the main man's mortality an open question. The actor who played Tony Soprano is incontrovertibly dead. But Tony? Let's review: James Gandolfini played a character on a TV show. Who wasn't a real human being. His character may or may not have made it out of the thrilling finale. Somewhere there are nincompoops with nothing better to do than debate his mortality, as if he were a living person. Or a dead one.

Oh, leave them alone, you say. *They're nincompoops—what do you expect?* Yes, but *why* are they nincompoops? I think it's because they're afraid of the ambiguous and the unresolved. And further, I think it's not just the nincompoops. I think we're all a bit afraid of ambiguity and irresolution. We long for closure; we work for resolution. If we can agree that Tony's dead, then we can move on. If we concur that he's still out there, marauding and killing and being all sensitive afterward, OK that can work too; Tony's alive, thank goodness. Either way, we feel better knowing. But *not* knowing: how will we sleep?

Improvised music challenges us to get over it. Overcome our collective anxiety about the ambiguous and the unresolved. Not because the music never gets tied up in a neat package—hey, that can happen sometimes—but because there are other forces at work, values other than clarity of message and tidy resolution, and in the process the music can leave you hanging. Free improvised music is rarely didactic. It comes without a concerted agenda. As a matter of fact, if the musicians come with their own individual game plan, it's generally dashed within a few minutes.*

Again, we're used to songs. Songs are rituals of tension and resolution. They stage anxiety only to eradicate it. They're little resolution machines. We're used to their basic mechanism—start up, grow a bit dissonant, move away from home, then race right back, landing on the tonal center or main theme.

Improvised music can resolve, for sure, but it tends to use other means. The musicians can exhaust an idea, working through the same material until it just feels finished, like wringing out a towel. They can take a journey, moving over the aforementioned peaks and valleys, concluding when the proverbial trip is over; that can come as relief, another sort of resolution. And there can be other, harder to describe kinds of resolutions, including situations in which musicians join together after having worked apart. Or they can end abruptly at the same instant, a seemingly impossible pinpoint

*Unless they are uncommonly powerful and force their plan on everyone else.

joint decision to stop, utilizing some of the ESP that Evan Parker alluded to.

What do we mean by ambiguity? Lack of clarity? Indecision? These are tricky areas, best broached by players who are the most seasoned contrarians, like Misha Mengelberg. When he flip-flops, moving one way then double thinking, it's accomplished at a meta-level, with a secret layer of confidence and assurance belying any superficial waffling. Mengelberg plays chess, and in chess it can be an advantage to appear confused. It's a kind of bluff. Playing fool to catch wise. When regular non-chess-playing folks are unclear, on the other hand, it's generally a disaster—it sends false messages to the other players, introducing rampant misunderstanding and general interaction dynamics meltdown. Being clear and decisive is the rule of thumb; other approaches are the exception.

But in a different way, instrumental music is almost always ambiguous. The ambiguity is ready-made. As a semiotic system, instrumental music is not designed to work semantically. It's not meaningless, but it doesn't make its meaning the way spoken or written language does. It's highly abstract. And that's a kind of ambiguity. As in: It is open to interpretation. It can be understood in multiple ways. And improvised music doubles down on that. As I said, it's not didactic. Because it is made jointly by people who haven't prearranged what they're going to say, it's not effective statement music. It's more like negotiation music. You hear the players in the process of making decisions, acting and reacting, mutually building, and playing something that hopefully has something unexpected in it. So in this way improvised music can be clear at the level of how it's made and ambiguous in terms of what a listener takes away.

Is that clear?

The Rule of Threes

Three is not only a prime number—it's the primo number. For improvised music, a three-way is pretty ideal. Triangulation has been a staple of jazz for years—think piano trio and the great three-somes of Sonny Rollins. It's a legacy of greatness that perseveres in free improvisation. I recommend seeking out lots of trios.

Why do trios work so well? Let's go step-by-step up the lineup ladder and assess:

1. Solo

Doubts can be raised about whether improvisation is even possible for a lone player. Is interaction an absolute necessity? Is playing alone actually a kind of composed music rather than improvisation? Solo playing can be fascinating, rich, quite complete in itself. It's inherently demonstrative—it's about *showing what you can do*—and can function like a lecture or a lesson, which is cool, for sure. John Zorn's stupendous 1980s solo music for saxophone, with its instantaneous shifts in timbre and volume and its startling nonlinear sense of unfolding, is a case in point. But you don't get the pleasure of hearing people working out the sounds together, which for me is half the fun.

One way to think about free solos as being genuinely improvised is to imagine that the kind of interaction one looks for between players is instead confined to the relationship between the soloist and the instrument or the performance context or the audience. Those contingencies can have a negotiated aspect just as provisional and unplanned as the kind we expect to find in the negotiations between different players in an ensemble.

2. Duet

Some of the finest improvisations ever played have been in this format. That said, there's an inherent obviousness about how things work, simply because there are two voices squaring off. Ping-Pong is a common metaphor: an idea is batted back and forth. It doesn't have to be like that, duos can be more oblique, but as a class they are burdened with dialogue's procedural tendency toward linear development and have to struggle to overcome that tilt.

3. Trio

Take the duet and add an X factor. Figuring out how the flow of ideas and sounds works in a trio is often difficult, but in the best hands it can be sublime communication. The third player adds exponentially to the possibilities, breaking up the linear flow and contributing layers of complexity. Duets are addition; trios are trigonometry. All three players can work together. Each player can work independently. Two can work together and the third can bugger off. Any of these proclivities can change multiple times over the course of an improvisation. It's much less polar, less dualistic. Another positive aspect: the trio has an approachable level of complexity. There's always some circling back and digging in. Rather than being factional, with players choosing sides, it tends to promote a kind of intimacy and intensity.

4. Quartet

Again, there have been some sensational ones, many of them, and there will be in the future, no doubt. But when there are four players, it can easily become double duets or a trio with a guest soloist. Or it can just slip into more conventional instrumental roles. Something about this format is automatically less concentrated with the addition of just one more person. But it's still a number with massive possibility for complexity and interplay, thrilling when well done.

5. Quintet+

Here we start to understand the general dictum that larger improvising ensembles have to be populated by really good improvisors. The main reason is that, unlike a duet or trio where everyone can easily hear everyone else, in a quintet it's more difficult to pay attention to the overall music (sometimes one player can't hear past another to grasp what a third one is doing!), and the results can be highly factional or segmented—two players here, three players here—with unsatisfactory or strained communication as an ensemble.* For topnotch players, this isn't a problem, and quintets or sextets, not to mention a group like the Peter Brötzmann Chicago Tentet or the London Improvisers Orchestra, can be jaw-dropping. It's like watching an Olympic diver: the degree of difficulty is so much higher that when it works, it's worth lots more points.

---

*Trumpeter Tom Djll formed his group Grosse Abfahrt specifically to push the issue of ensemble size, assembling a larger ensemble of eight to ten players. "This range seems to settle in a locale where there is a strong opportunity for individual sound-agents to emerge and make a statement against the ensemble backdrop, and also for the entire ensemble to cohere into long-form structures that transcend the productions of conventional improvised music sociality." From Djll's liner notes to Grosse Abfahrt, *Vanity* (Emanem Records, 2009).

Dancing Between the Hypothetical Poles

For just a moment, allow yourself to entertain a question: What is improvised and what is not? Careful, it's a deep rabbit hole, and if you get hung up on it, you might lose interest in listening to the music. But it's a topic worth flirting with, at least asking what is the threshold or theoretical border between improvisation and something else. I propose two poles, each hypothetical.

1. Everything is improvised
2. Nothing is improvised.

Let's draw it out a bit on both ends.

In theory, you could say that anything that involves a decision has some uncertainty in it, and if it's uncertain and requires a decision, the agent making that decision has to weigh all the factors at hand at any given moment and then choose. So, think of a pianist playing a piece of composed music, with strict directives covering tempo and dynamics; everything is preplanned. Still, when playing the piece, in every instant, the pianist has to *decide* to continue playing the score and how closely. In every instant, she could deviate and play something totally different. Or stop. Or play a different instrument. Or sing. Whatever. The world is profoundly open, a nonstop improvisation, free of constraint and ultimately enriched with will. Anything can happen in any way at any time if you want it to. A phenomenology of conjured experience, everything is boiled down to desire, and actions are just manifestations of real-time choosing. Life is navigated by means of improvisation alone.

Or you could opt for a deeply paranoid view that holds in contempt any suggestion of free will. Nothing is improvised because nobody actually has a choice; everything is mapped out in some frighteningly detailed way. Imagine from this perspective that a musician who thinks he's improvising is first of all personally unenlightened, deluded into imagining that decisions about how to proceed are made by him, when in truth he's programmed to make those decisions. Always, at every level, without exception. He and his trio play some wild music, seemingly free—ha! Their freedom is a simulacrum of liberty, every move as predictable as one in a game of checkers. No surprises. In fact, the very notion of surprise is an unreality. From the selection of instrument to the specific material played in a given context, everything is part of a completely orchestrated, calculable cosmos.

In practice, these are impossible hypothetical poles; all real music lies somewhere in between. But I have an exercise for you, a sort of perverse workshop to test their plausibility and hone your skills as a listener. First, attend a concert of composed music adopting a firmly held conviction that everything is improvised. Listen to each note with this in mind, imagining the performer's sweat as evidence of a difficult set of choices, constantly wondering what the player will do next. Then go to a concert of freely improvised music with the mind-set that nothing is improvised, all freedom is complete folly, and the players are puppets on strings. Once you've explored these extremes, you should be able to better see how the music shuttles between willed invention, codified formula, and some hard-to-define collective creation.

Poly-Free

Q: What is the free improvisor free from?
A: Editorial oversight.
Q: What is the free improvisor free to do?
A: Whatever the party calls for.

A big tree branch falls into a mountain stream. The flowing water pools up above it; below it the current slows to a trickle. After some time, the stream diverts around the branch. Bits of refuse join the impediment—leaves, smaller branches, assorted mountain gunk. The stream widens and deepens where it meets the wood. So, is the stream less *free* because of the branch?

Obviously not. It's not a matter of freedom; the stream is now different. Maybe, if this goes on for long enough, the stream won't be a stream anymore, and perhaps the branch won't be a branch. Then we'll talk about a lake and a dam. It would cast things in a very different light if we were to frame this event around a discussion of the relative freedom of the stream and the branch. That would lend the whole scene an air of righteousness, an urgent sense of justice, as if the free flow of the stream should be fought for and the branch was an antagonist. No need. The stream and branch are transformed when they come together, but it's not about freedom. Music that uses improvisation but also has composed or preconceived sections is not more or less free than freely improvised music, certainly not in any ontological way, but the nature of the two is quite different.

Leaving the hypothetical poles for the real world, we find that, in fact, there are scads of players who utilize one or another hybrid of improvisation and composition, drawing elements or strategies or game plans from both and applying them within the course of a single piece. Steve

Lacy spoke of his transition from what he called the "hermetic-free" of total improvisation, which he explored in depth in the 1960s, to something he termed "poly-free." This could entail any combination at all of unpremeditated interplay, fully scored music with melodies and rhythms and harmony, graphic scores, vague verbal directions, games, role-playing, or the use of a conductor. Any approach is admissible in poly-free music.

The impetus in Lacy's case came from the creeping feeling he had that there was starting to be a "correct" way to freely improvise, that expectations were mounting and an aesthetic was developing, and that this was fastening at least into a routine, perhaps even into a protocol. To break out of the trap, he decided to admit predetermined materials back into what he did. With poly-free, Lacy wanted to allow the music to be free *not* to be free.*

---

*In 1988 the cellist Tom Cora told me that he'd grown weary of the tendency to "avoid" in free improvisation—avoiding tunes, beat, harmony, standard technique. His response was to include all these things in his free improvising much more liberally, quoting from eastern European folk music, using a loop to make little rhythms or set up simple harmonic backdrops.

I have chosen to concentrate on free improvisation in this listener's guide because all the
most difficult aspects of coming to the music as a
new audience member are addressed in a hyper-
concentrated way there. If you can learn what to
listen for in purely improvised music, you'll have
no trouble finding applications of those listening skills in the realm of the poly-free. And you
are heartily encouraged to do so. For instance, the
music of the previously mentioned Henry Threadgill band utilizes hybrid approaches as a matter of
course, as does the music of many figures who also
enjoy free improvising. The door back and forth is
never locked. Often it's left wide open.

The freedom to be free and also not to be free
is naturally an ideal situation. But let's also take
caution when we think about how these categories
function as explored together. Free improvised
music can be instigated without any preplanning,
no discussion or blueprint, sometimes without any
sense of even a basic idea about how the music will
proceed. As with the branch and the stream, that
doesn't make it more or less "free"; it's just one way

of working. On the other hand, little incursions into the supposed freedom of the music often happen. Someone asks: Should we play one long piece or several pieces? Or a thoughtful player warns her colleagues that the audience is here to see the rock band they're opening up for, so they might be restless, noisy, and inattentive. One wouldn't say that these small comments taint the music, making it impure—that's stupid and dogmatic. But it's also ignoring the obvious not to recognize that this pre-show input might change the way the players play.

This is something to bear in mind when listening to music in which there are sections of open improvising—no directions, no score—as part of a poly-free piece. The improvisation that happens in that section is not exactly the same as music freely improvised by the same participants outside of the domain of the composed music. The preconceived parts always influence the improvising, often by actually changing what someone chooses to play (they can't help but have the other music in mind), but if by no other means then by putting the free play into a context.

Free improvisation is its own discipline, just like composing. And the two can be brought together fruitfully, as we know from the history of jazz and many kinds of traditional and classical music from around the world, in which improvisation is a tool that a performer uses in navigating written or conventionalized music. When I put on a masterpiece of poly-free music, like Julius Hemphill's *Dogon A.D.*, I am listening for the way the players negotiate these two worlds, the interweaving of strategies that celebrate both the individual will of the player and the global vision of the composer. Duke Ellington was already composing music with this in mind in the 1920s, and you can do no better than listening to his 1940 piece "Concerto for Cootie" to hear trumpeter Cootie Williams balance the needs of the orchestra and his own personal statement, Ellington's score serving as both prompt and guardrail.

For a more contemporary example, find some music by the Tobias Delius Quartet. The Dutch have taken hybridity to a very special place, largely under the influence of Misha Mengelberg, in which compositions are sometimes incorporated wholesale into the act of free improvising. This may sound like a contradiction, but somehow in Misha's hands it works. There's a whole raft of bands in which the lines between free and preset material are made willfully fuzzy—I'm thinking of the Ab Baars Trio, Available Jelly, the Eric Boeren Quartet, the bands of the late lamented Sean Bergin, the Corkestra, Joost Buis & Astronotes, and of course Mengelberg's own ICP (Instant Composers Pool) Orchestra.

Now for contrast, listen to some other poly-free explorers. Start with well-documented younger bandleaders Ken Vandermark and Ellery Eskelin—diverse ideas from two big thinkers, brilliant and expansive. Now move up in age, back to Anthony Braxton, whose oeuvre could occupy a lifetime of listening, and Wadada Leo Smith, another intrepid hybridist who invented a whole system called Ankhrasmation for the improvised interpretation of his scores. And don't leave out Mr. Lacy from your survey of the hybridists; start with music from the 1970s, when he was a sponge for different resources. To do justice to all these different approaches, even just to cursorily introduce them, would take another book altogether, *A Listener's Guide to Creative Music*.

As a start, try to listen for the spots where you can clearly hear that what the musicians are playing is precomposed, and when you can—this is more difficult—discern the places in which improvisation is occurring without being steered externally. If you can't quite tell, that's interesting in itself. Beyond this, you'll have to investigate what each specific composer/bandleader is doing, which can be as different from one another as are free improvisors. In fact, there could be field books just for some of the most prolific of the poly-free, *A Listener's Guide to Muhal Richard Abrams* or *A Listener's Guide to Tim Berne*.

A final note: the term "freedom" has been the source of many misconceptions in improvised music, and it's helpful to keep from investing in the word too deeply. Of course, giant philosophical debates rage around the topic, and in the wrong hands "free" music can be rallied around as a facile and softheaded notion, much the way that the term "anarchy" gets bandied about in the dopier environs of popular culture, as if it means doing whatever you please without regard for others.

Sun Ra, one of the early masters of poly-free music, was ultimately skeptical of the rhetoric of freedom. He preferred the terms "discipline" and "precision," emphasizing that the wildest-seeming music, if played well, requires the implementation of both these concepts. The point isn't determining what's free and what's not. It's time better spent paying attention to what's going on in the music and how it's made. Free improvisation is a method for making music; it isn't an independent value or quality. Knowing if the music is spontaneously improvised or if it is an interpretation of someone's preconceived idea is worthwhile. Judging it solely based on that knowledge is not.

Kindling II: 20 Classic Poly-Free Records

1. Sun Ra & His Solar Arkestra, *The Magic City*
2. Muhal Richard Abrams, *Mama and Daddy*
3. Art Ensemble of Chicago, *A Jackson in Your House*
4. ICP Orchestra, *Aan & Uit*
5. Anthony Braxton, *Quartet (Dortmund) 1976*
6. London Jazz Composers Orchestra, *Ode*
7. Wadada Leo Smith, *Kabell Years: 1971–1979*
8. Steve Lacy, *Scratching the Seventies/Dreams*
9. Henry Threadgill Zooid, *This Brings Us to Volume 2*
10. John Carter, *Fields*
11. Julius Hemphill, *Dogon A.D.*
12. Anthony Davis, *Epistēmē*
13. John Zorn, *Archery*

14. Frank Lowe & Eugene Chadbourne, *Don't Punk Out*
15. Joe Morris Quartet, *Balance*
16. William Parker & The Little Huey Creative Music Orchestra, *Raincoat in the River*
17. Tim Berne, *Tim Berne's Fractured Fairy Tales*
18. Ellery Eskelin/Andrea Parkins/Jim Black, *The Secret Museum*
19. Tobias Delius 4-Tet, *Pelikanismus*
20. Vandermark 5, *Beat Reader*

Distraction and Sleep

The equivalent of Eagle Scout status in improvised music listening is awarded for a listener's
capacity to get something from the proceedings
whilst asleep . . . or damned close. You think I'm
joking, but I'm being dead serious. Some of the
most memorable moments for me have come just
as consciousness was reclaiming my limp brain,
my body jerking awake after having nodded off. If
you've reached a certain level, like some high lamas
or drunken masters, the general rules don't apply
and you can process the music while fast asleep.

Part of this has to do with what goes on at the
edge of wakefulness, via beta waves and hypnagogic

hallucinations. Full concentration, which is the A1 rule for most listeners, is only effective for hearing 90 percent of what's going on in the music. The rest is accessible in the altered state of distraction or near sleep, the dozy zone between being totally blacked out and being awake. For me, it's the same mental space in which, early in the morning, I remember where I left my keys or I think of a word I was trying to remember the day before. Whatever brain gremlins were holding those thoughts hostage are caught unawares, and they give up the goods.

Simple distractedness can work too. I warn you off this in the early going when it's much more effective to come to a concert fresh-faced and ready to concentrate. But once you've been at it for a stretch, you may find that dropping your focus can reward you in ways you hadn't expected. You'll notice things that were previously inaccessible. It takes a level of confidence and mega-relaxation, something that places you in the upper echelon of improvised music fans; if you're guarded or feeling guilty about letting your mind wander, the tech-

nique just won't work. But whether you're emerging from a dream or just not paying attention, if
you can master this counterintuitive technique, it
will yield some special experiences, allowing prob-
ing associations between whatever you're thinking
about and the music at hand and producing the
overall surreal matrix where lived and imagined
realities can mix and match.

It's important to keep a couple of things in
mind, however, in experimenting with this advanced method of listenership:

1. When you are asleep, you run the risk of calling
   attention to yourself and away from the music, if
   you should, for example, crash to the floor, snore
   with your head thrown back, or drool.
2. In fact, if you are a champion snorer or sleep-talker,
   don't even try this technique.
3. Avoid sitting where the musicians can see you.
   Sleeping is generally not taken as a gesture of
   respect.

Thinking and Chewing Gum (at the Same Time)

Here's an exercise to help you empathize with the improvisor. Go to the top of a flight of stairs. Make sure they're carpeted. Start to walk down them, and while you're in motion, look at your feet and think about the fact that you're walking down the stairs.

It's tough, right? The thoughts somehow get underfoot. Your stride gets tangled. Self-awareness becomes self-consciousness, and in the process you lose your god-given groove. The familiar act of descending the stairs becomes clunky and alien, even dangerous. It's the same as what they say about balancing on the high wire: don't look down, don't think about it too much, just walk.

This experience of temporal-spatial disorientation may help explain something about how thinking works in improvised music. It's really pretty hard to think about improvising while you're doing it. Mats Gustafsson told me that the reason he worked so hard to have his technique in shape—insane hours spent practicing, experimenting, cultivating, and honing new material—isn't to be able to play impressively; it's necessary prep to reduce the time it takes to get from an impulse to an action. Thinking is *way* too slow to do this. Improvisors need to have hammer-on-knee reactions, instantaneous decisions, reflexes not contemplations.

Get a record of improvised music. Listen through one of the tracks a few times to get familiar with it. Now try listening to it with an ear toward discerning the places where one of the improvisors is *thinking*. You can hear it pretty clearly sometimes—an idea pops into the head, and they change direction or they introduce something new or make a big statement. It's not necessarily a negative thing, but it tends to be structural rather than substantive. And it can't happen for too long or too many times, lest the quickness and fluidity become bogged down and pedantic. Improvisation mired in thought, in *deliberation*, is generally not so fun or fulfilling.

One interesting counterexample was a group that the Dutch reed player Peter van Bergen led in the '90s called Loos. He composed material for the players, quite extreme in one way or another—in register or in dynamic or in intensity or something like that. The players were supposed to introduce short bursts of extremist music, then fall silent for an interval, during which they would think about what they'd done, deciding which material to play next. This, van Bergen figured, is where the improvisation happened, in the very act of choosing what to play next. So you didn't hear the improvising as sound, you heard it as silence, and then you heard the results of the improvised choices made by the players. You literally heard them thinking. It had a nice contrary spirit to it and produced some very decisive music, but it was an anomaly, I think, that proves the rule.

Improvisors who look down usually fall.

You and the Night and the Music: Audience Participation

The jazz saxophonist Von Freeman once told me he'd been working on a book for fifty years. His topic? The audience. From the bandstand, he figured, you had a vantage better than most sociologists on human behavior. But he also told me he had not cracked the audience's code. Experimenting for all those years, he still couldn't say with any certainty what made them tick. The audience is the ultimate wild card. It has an impact, no doubt, but it's hard to say exactly what that impact is and how it is communicated—except, of course, in the rare cases when someone in the crowd makes a spectacle of themselves. I've seen that happen a few times. It amps up the tension, makes all the forces of energy in a room become suddenly palpable.

A little label called Bead Records run by the guitarist Peter Cusack once put out two volumes titled *Groups in Front of People*. These LPs culled live recordings by several free-improvising ensembles. Cusack explained that the selection of tracks reflected the interest in "the group audience relation and how this [a]ffects particular performances."*

Over the course of a few cuts, several archetypes of said relation are explored. First there was a particularly attentive crowd, listening quietly, which allowed the band to enjoy long silences in the middle of pieces. Then there was a small, somewhat ill-suited bar in which the air-conditioning was loud and the people weren't paying attention. Cusack: "It seemed to me that through the combination of the place and a small but rather indifferent audience, the group tended to close in and make music for itself." Another set was at a jazz venue in Rotterdam in which "the music had gradually

---

*Peter Cusack, liner notes to *Groups in Front of People* (Bead Records, 1979).

moved from the stage to include the whole room." Cusack continues: "The audience is really enjoying the give and take, in which the squeaking door, chinking glasses and other noises are all part."

The final example came from a concert at a theater in Delft. Cusack describes it nicely:

A celebration was in progress when we arrived and there was a long wait before starting. Our audience was people remaining from the celebration, people there for the music and people there because almost everything else was closed. Those who wanted to listen did so, the rest carried on with their conversations. The music was not particularly popular and a definite feeling of hostility grew up. This greatly affected the way the group played. Normally many disparate and separate musical lines occurred within the group, but on this occasion the situation forced us much closer together. As a whole it was the most integrated concert that we played.

The *Groups in Front of People* field study verges on social science, which is appropriate, since freely improvised music is so sensitive to changes in atmosphere, especially concerning the audience. In my years of organizing improvised music concerts and fretting over audience noise, I came to regard the audience's "performance" with nearly as much scrutiny as the players'. There were good audiences, which were not always the quietest but were always respectful and attentive; there were bad audiences, which did not always result in inferior music but forced the hand of the musicians in one way or another. A loud ambience of any kind makes it difficult to play very softly. But radio silence can also signal boredom or apathy, neither of which cycles into the audience-group feedback loop in a generative way.

You can become a connoisseur of musician-audience relations. The first step is to look for the place where, outside of special situations, that communication is audible: when pieces end. This is a special moment, when the musicians all agree that an improvisation is over and the audience is invited to applaud. Or boo. Or throw tomatoes. Or confetti. Money. Whatever. If the spirit moves, the crowd may express it. This is when you can sense

most vividly the transactional relationship between players and listeners—what they each give
and take from the shared experience. For a period
when I booked a long-standing series at the same
venue, one fellow used to come regularly. We knew
him from the final moments of an improvisation,
when, before the last note had died out, a percus-
sive noise would declare the music finished. When
we finally figured out what was going on, we called
him the Clicker. He had a nearly pathological fear
of the end of the music, which he would signal by
clicking his tongue against the roof of his mouth.
I found it dictatorial. The Clicker alone would decide when the music was done. But he also brought
sensationally delicious coconut macaroons, which
he shared liberally with all comers, so that almost
made up for his microcosmic power trip.

From its endpoints, you can move back into
the heart of the musical performance in search
of player-audience interaction: nodding heads,
squinted eyes, a look of ecstasy or revulsion, sometimes an involuntary whoop or holler, and maybe
a concomitant reaction from the players, a regis-

tration that they are aware of the quality of their listenership. Audiences in different places have varying customs, too. In New Orleans, one concert organizer cultivated a very loud and interactive atmosphere that was closer to a hootenanny than a chamber concert. On the other end of the spectrum, I once booked an ultra-quiet band at a festival on the stage of a rock club; the audience collectively held its breath, but the bar's cat, unaware that music was being played, ventured onstage, moved between the players, and began swatting at the cellist's slowly moving bow. At that point, the crowd exploded with laughter, catharsis just in the nick of time.

Additional Reading: Seven Great Books (Plus One DVD)

1. Kevin Whitehead, *New Dutch Swing*
2. Edwin Prévost, *No Sound Is Innocent: AMM and the Practice of Self-Invention/Meta-Musical Narratives/Essays*
3. George E. Lewis, *A Power Stronger than Itself: The AACM and American Experimental Music*
4. Derek Bailey, *Improvisation: Its Nature and Practice in Music*
5. Nathaniel Mackey, *Djbot Baghostus's Run*
6. Leo Smith, *Notes (8 Pieces) Source a New World Music: Creative Music*

7. Joe Morris, *Perpetual Frontier: The Properties of Free Music*

8. Bernard Josse, *Soldier of the Road: A Portrait of Peter Brötzmann* (DVD)

A Little Rouge,
a Touch of Blush

Before he switched from playing improvised bass
to composing contemporary classical music, Maar-
ten Altena once expressed an idea to me that has
kept me thinking ever since. Already veering away
from free music, he said that the thing that concerned him was what he called the "cosmetics of
improvisation." Instantly, I knew what he meant.
It's the same suspicion that Steve Lacy had when
he invented the term "poly-free." If you attend lots
of concerts of free improvisation, you begin to recognize certain moves that might be considered
staples of the music. If it's approached uncritically,
improvising can be quite routine; if it's driven by

the quest for a particular sound, rather than by an interactive process, it can become reified. That was Altena's worry: that the music had developed a specific aesthetic, a way that it was *supposed* to sound, which is a superficial aspect. At its worst, he contended, the musicians stop improvising and play in a terribly mannered way, trying to match the sounds that they think of as sounding like improvised music.

What this sets up for us advanced technicians is a perilous task: to distinguish the "real" music from the "cosmetic" music. It certainly requires the most detailed analysis and the brightest and most acute listening. And even so, I'm not sure I am equipped to suggest any surefire, infallible bullshit detector capable of parsing the actual from the imitative. There's plenty of music that "sounds like" improvisation because it is made by improvising. But Altena was on to something important and truthful, that there can be too much emphasis on the preciousness of the sounds and too little on the mechanism through which they've been made. This is why we've spent the bulk of this little book on interaction dynamics; that's where the unexpected things happen, and in human interplay the desired sound is only forged by means of a negotiation, a set of agreements and disagreements. When there's only agreement, and the agreement has to do with the intended sound of the music, then there's no tension and no development, and the music slackens. Does that mean it's not improvised? I don't know and don't really care. What it definitely means is that I'm less interested in the music, however it was made.

On the Moral Superiority of Improvised Music

It isn't.

I find sanctimonious free-music followers un-
bearable. Improvised music is not better than
other kinds of music. It has a long symbiotic relationship with various species of popular and classical music from around the world, and in most
cases its practitioners are respectful of those different traditions. Some of them could be classi-
fied as super-fans of other types of music, collect-
ing and cataloging and learning as much as they
can about other lineages. I think of saxophonist
Michael Moore, who has a magnificent collection
of ethnographic recordings and who knows more

than many ethnomusicologists about diverse traditions, including jazz. He's got an encyclopedic knowledge of Duke Ellington's music, which has come in handy playing with the ICP Orchestra.

The improvised music fans I find most attractive are those who recognize connections between free improvisation and, say, dub reggae, serial composition, and Malagasy *valiha* music, let alone dominant traditions that directly involve other idioms of improvisation, like Indian or Iranian classical music. Our duty, as listeners, is to be restlessly curious, to root around this big globe and dig up new things to fill our ears and minds. It's more a matter of being inquisitive than of being eclectic. If you blinder yourself to that inquisitiveness in allegiance to some ideal of itchy, scratchy *plink* and *plonk*, you've lost the gambit. In fact, if you find yourself leaning that way, you have an assignment: go find something else to listen to. Eating dark green veggies is good for you, but if you eat nothing else, you'll get sick and die. Same here for free improvisation.

So improvised music is not morally (or aesthetically or procedurally) superior. But I do think it's important to recognize what is special about it, not to be absolutely and unthinkingly relativistic. Indeed, my position on its global relevance has been solidifying over the last couple of decades, and now I feel strongly that free improvisation will eventually be seen as one of the great contributions of Western society to world culture, on par with cubism's introduction of multiple-point perspective or abstraction's renewed attention to materiality and plasticity over observation and representation. What those early twentieth-century artistic concepts opened up in terms of image, vision, and form, improvised music has cracked open in terms of time. It's so much more than spontaneous outpourings of emotion or a brash proclamation that "I can do anything I want"; improvised music has contributed something deeply profound to the world, a new way of thinking about sound and space and temporal experience and personal interaction.

Life List: A Selected Checklist of Major Living Free Improvisors

Reeds:

Anker, Lotte

Baars, Ab

Berne, Tim

Bevan, Tony

Boykin, David

Braxton, Anthony

Brötzmann, Peter

Brown, Rob

Butcher, John

Carl, Rüdiger

Charles, Xavier

Delius, Tobias

Derome, Jean

Dunmall, Paul

Ehrlich, Marty

Eskelin, Ellery

Ewart, Douglas

Falzone, James

Floridis, Floros

Freedman, Lori

Fuchs, Wolfgang

Gayle, Charles

Goldberg, Ben

Golia, Vinny

Gregorio, Guillermo

Guralnick, Tom

Gustafsson, Mats

Jaume, André

Klapper, Martin

Koch, Hans

Laubrock, Ingrid

Lazro, Daunik

Leimgruber, Urs

Ljungkvist, Fredrik

Mahall, Rudi

Malaby, Tony

McPhee, Joe

Mitchell, Roscoe

Moore, Michael

Oswald, John

Parker, Evan

Pavone, Jessica

Rempis, Dave

Roberts, Matana

Rothenberg, Ned

Sakata, Akiri

Sclavis, Louis

Sehnaoui, Christine

Stetson, Colin

Van Bergen, Peter

Vandermark, Ken

Ward, Alex

Watts, Trevor

Williams, Mars

Zorn, John

Flute:

Denley, Jim

Dick, Robert

Mitchell, Nicole

Shakuhachi:

Bell, Clive

Trumpet/Cornet:

Berman, Josh

Broo, Magnus

Bynum, Taylor H.

Djll, Tom

Dörner, Axel
Evans, Peter
Hautzinger, Franz
Heberer, Thomas
Kondo, Toshinori
Mazurek, Rob
Provan, Felicity
Robertson, Herb
Smith, Wadada Leo
Ulher, Birgit
Wooley, Nate

Trombone/Tuba:

Anderson, Ray
Bauer, Johannes
Bauer, Konrad
Bishop, Jeb
Brand, Gail
Buis, Joost
Christmann, Günter
Holmlander, Per-Åke
Hubweber, Paul

Lewis, George
Malfatti, Radu
Marshall, Oren
Poore, Melvyn
Swell, Steve
Tomlinson, Alan
Tramontana, Sebi
Wierbos, Wolter
Wilkinson, Alan

Piano:

Abrams, Muhal Richard
Baker, Jim
Beresford, Steve
Burn, Chris
Courvoisier, Sylvie
Crispell, Marilyn
Davis, Kris
Demierre, Jacques
Fernández, Agustí
Fuhler, Cor
Gräwe, Georg

Gumpert, Ulrich
Iyer, Vijay
Karayorgis, Pandelis
Kaufmann, Achim
Mengelberg, Misha
Reason, Dana
Sandell, Sten
Schweizer, Irène
Schlippenbach,
    Alexander von
Takase, Aki
Taylor, Cecil
Thomas, Pat
Tilbury, John
Tippett, Keith
Van Hove, Fred
Weston, Veryan

Accordion:

Parkins, Andrea

Vibes:

Adasiewicz, Jason

Cello:

Friedlander, Erik
Honsinger, Tristan
Lee, Okkyung
Lee, Peggy
Levin, Daniel
Lonberg-Holm, Fred
Mattos, Marcio
Reid, Tomeka
Reijseger, Ernst
Schütz, Martin
Veliotis, Nikos

Violin:

Feldman, Mark
Hallett, Sylvia
Hug, Charlotte
Kolkowski, Aleks
    (Stroh instruments)
Maneri, Mat
Oliver, Mary
Paulson, Jen Clare
Rose, Jon

Smith, LaDonna

Wachsmann, Philipp

Zingaro, Carlos

Synthesizer/
Electronics:

Barrett, Peter

Casserley, Lawrence

Drumm, Kevin

Labycz, Brian

Lehn, Thomas

Marhaug, Lasse

Merzbow (Masama Akita)

Mori, Ikue

Müller, Günter

Obermayer, Paul

Perkis, Tim

Prati, Walter

Ryan, Joel

Vecci, Marco

Turntable:

Dieb13

DJ Sniff

Marclay, Christian

Yoshihide, Otomo

Voice:

Blonk, Jaap

Gilbert, Jodi

Hirsch, Shelley

Jauniaux, Catherine

Mackness, Vanessa

Minton, Phil

Nicols, Maggie

Guitar:

Akchoté, Noël

Boni, Raymond

Chadbourne, Eugene

Cline, Nels

Frith, Fred

Haino, Keiji

Halvorson, Mary

Hessels, Terrie
Kaiser, Henry
Lussier, René
Moor, Andy
Moore, Thurston
Morris, Joe
Munthe, Christian
O'Rourke, Jim
Parker, Jeff
Rowe, Keith
Russell, John
Stackenäs, David
Williams, Davey
Wittwer, Stephan

Pipa:
Xiao-Fen, Min

Harp:
Davies, Rhodri
LeBaron, Anne
Parkins, Zeena

Hurdy-Gurdy:
Wishart, Stevie

Koto:
Masaoka, Miya
Yagi, Michiyo

Invented/Found Instruments:
Bohman, Adam
Klapper, Martin
Rammel, Hal

Bass:
Abrams, Joshua
Bauer, Matthias
Berthling, Johan
De Joode, Wilbert
Dresser, Mark
Edwards, John
Fell, Simon H.
Flaten, Ingebrigt Håker

Glerum, Ernst

Gray, Darin

Guy, Barry

Hébert, John

Helias, Mark

Kessler, Kent

Léandre, Joëlle

Lightcap, Chris

Lindberg, John

Manderscheid, Dieter

McBride, Nate

Müller, Torsten

Parker, William

Phillips, Barre

Pliakas, Marino

Roebke, Jason

Rogers, Paul

Turetzky, Bertram

Drums:

Bennink, Han

Black, Jim

Cleaver, Gerald

Corsano, Chris

Daisy, Tim

Drake, Hamid

Fujiwara, Tomas

Graves, Milford

Hauser, Fritz

Hemingway, Gerry

Hession, Paul

Johansson, Sven-Åke

Kotche, Glenn

Lovens, Paul

Lytton, Paul

Moholo-Moholo, Louis

Nilssen-Love, Paal

Ninh, Lê Quan

Noble, Steve

Nordeson, Kjell

Oxley, Tony

Prévost, Eddie

Reed, Mike

Robair, Gino

Rosaly, Frank

Sanders, Mark

Sommer, Günter "Baby"

Strid, Raymond

Studer, Fredy

Taylor, Chad

Tsuchitori, Toshi

Turner, Roger

van der Schyff, Dylan

Vatcher, Michael

Walter, Weasel

Wertmüller, Michael

Zerang, Michael